Twayne's United States Authors Series

Sylvia E. Bowman, *Editor*

INDIANA UNIVERSITY

John P. Marquand

JOHN P. MARQUAND

by JOHN J. GROSS
Bowling Green State University

(TUSAS) 33

Twayne Publishers, Inc.   ::   New York

MANUFACTURED IN THE UNITED STATES OF AMERICA BY
UNITED PRINTING SERVICES, INC.
NEW HAVEN, CONN.

FOR TULA

Contents

Preface

WHATEVER MAY BE the final critical judgment of later generations upon the work of John Phillips Marquand, there is no question today that he was the most widely read, successful novelist of his time. He was the professional of professionals. He was, further, by almost unanimous consent and agreement, the only seriously regarded social novelist of his era. Not that there were no unfavorable critical judgments upon his work. He wrote well, most critics agreed; indeed, he wrote almost too well; and, while admired for his ironic treatment of his materials, he could be termed by a critic like Maxwell Geismar as a writer who substituted this quality of irony for such qualities as "the intellectual boldness of the major writers, the moral hardness, and the depth insights."

In the novels of contemporary American life, from the publication of *The Late George Apley* (1937) through his last novel, *Women and Thomas Harrow* (1958), Marquand spoke as truly of the changing social patterns of the twentieth century as was possible for a writer of keen sensibility and acute powers of observation. He became, in truth, a mine of information about social attitudes—a mine worked increasingly by the sociologists of this generation.

While Marquand has been widely read, there has not been a close critical examination or appreciation of his major work before this one. I have therefore gone into considerably more detail in relating the action of the novels than would perhaps be necessary for a later critic of Marquand. The pages which follow trace the career of John P. Marquand from the publication of *The Late George Apley* through the serious novels written during the last twenty-five years of his life. I have not chosen to review the work of the first fifteen of his productive years when he wrote as best he knew how for the popular, mass-circulation magazines. Written during an apprenticeship for which serious critics have forgiven him, none of these novels before his Pulitzer Prize-winning *Apley* has anything significant to say about the kind of novelist Marquand became. Although the reader might well explore his popular magazine fiction in the collection of short stories published in the 1954 volume entitled *Thirty Years*, this exploration would tell him little about the novels introduced to the reading public with the *Apley* memoir.

If no explanation is required for the study which I have attempted, perhaps a word of apology should be spoken to the Apleys and their descendants, and to other patrician New Englanders and proper Bostonians, by me, an adopted son of the Middle West, and the descendant of a long line of Oregon New Englanders, several generations removed, who has the temerity to be the first to report upon their lives and, more particularly, upon the life and work of their creator, Mr. John Phillips Marquand. For Mr. Marquand *was* very nearly a Bostonian, despite a certain amount of rather small-minded opinion to the contrary, owing to the unfortunate fact of his having been born in Wilmington, Delaware.

Friends and associates have been generous in their criticism and advice, particularly Professor Victor M. Bogle who read the manuscript and gave valuable suggestions for its improvement. Mr. William Bellis, though no admirer of Marquand's work, aided me in arriving at certain critical judgments. Sylvia E. Bowman, generous friend and editor of extraordinary thoroughness, has given me needed encouragement and indispensable assistance. I am grateful to the graduate division of Indiana University which provided a grant-in-aid, enabling me to complete my manuscript and to prepare it for the publisher. I acknowledge with gratitude the permission of Little, Brown and Company to quote from the works of John Phillips Marquand. Harcourt, Brace and Company generously permitted me to quote briefly from *Babbitt* by Sinclair Lewis and from *The Cocktail Party* by T. S. Eliot.

JOHN J. GROSS

Indiana University
Kokomo Campus

Chronology

1893 November 10, John P. Marquand born in Wilmington, Delaware, the descendant of such worthies as Joseph Dudley, Margaret Fuller, and Edward Everett Hale.

1907 Attended school at Newburyport while living with three maiden aunts at Curzon's Mill.

1911 Received scholarship to Harvard for majors in scientific subjects after having been rejected by local Harvard Club.

1914 Though he intensely disliked his major in chemistry, he finished all his courses in three years and left Harvard to find work in the summer, 1914.

1915 Returned to receive degree at Harvard with the class of 1915. Marquand lived in a boarding house at Harvard (run by two maiden ladies) called "Miss Mooney's Pleasure Palace." From his fourth-floor room he sometimes engaged James B. Conant, later president of Harvard, in water-bag fights on the stairs. While at Harvard in his last year, Marquand invited to attend Professor Copeland's "Tuesday Night Readings." Felt first stirrings of literary ambitions. Made *Lampoon* but no other clubs or societies.

1916 Spent year on Boston *Transcript* as reporter at $15.00 per week, before raise to $25.00.

1917- To Texas with Battery A of the Massachusetts National
1918 Guard for duty on Mexican border. In April left for officer's training camp at Plattsburg. Commissioned first lieutenant in August, 1917. Overseas with Fourth Division; intelligence officer with 77th artillery.

1919- Went to work for New York *Herald-Tribune*, wrote
1920 features for the Sunday magazine. Recommended to the J. Walter Thompson advertising agency by the late Robert Benchley when he expressed a desire to make more money. Picked up the background for the experiences of H. M. Pulham. Worked in Lifebuoy soap campaign.

1921-
1922   Decided to write a novel on $400 saved. Retired to old mill building at Curzon's Mill. Turned out an unspeakable novel titled *The Unspeakable Gentleman,* purchased by the *Ladies' Home Journal* for $2,000, perhaps because, as was later said, the magazine needed a historical novel to prove the quality of its new color presses. On the strength of this initial success, Marquand wrote and sold short pieces to George Horace Lorimer of the *Saturday Evening Post* and to Ray Long of *Cosmopolitan.* Something like a competition developed for the Marquand product.

1922   On September 8, married Christine Sedgwick (of the *Atlantic Monthly* Sedgwicks) in Stockbridge, Massachusetts. Lived in Cambridge, Mass.

1923   John P. Marquand, Jr. born. *Four of a Kind.*

1925   *The Black Cargo. Lord Timothy Dexter,* a historical study of the Newburyport eccentric of the Federalist period; restudied in the last book Marquand was to write.

1927   Christine, first daughter born. Marquand busy with the writing of short fiction for the "slicks."

1930   *Warning Hill,* a novel suggesting the major ones to follow.

1934   *Ming Yellow.*

1935   *No Hero.* Marquand divorced by Christine Marquand at Pittsfield, Massachusetts, May 19. At the recommendation of his editors, Marquand then traveled in China to obtain material for *Post* serials. Met Adelaide Hooker in China.

1936   Engagement to Adelaide Hooker following his return from China. *Thank You, Mr. Moto,* first fruit of his travels in the Orient. Purchased home at Kent's Island, near Newburyport.

1937   Marriage to Adelaide Hooker at her parents' apartment on Park Avenue in New York, April 16. *The Late George Apley,* first of his serious social novels; *Think Fast, Mr. Moto,* second fruits of his travel abroad.

1938   *Mr. Moto So Sorry.* Marquand awarded the Pulitzer Prize for *Apley.*

1939   *Wickford Point,* Marquand's second novel in his twentieth-century *Comedie Humaine.*

1940   Blanch Ferry Marquand born.

1941 *H. M. Pulham, Esquire.* Marquand returned to army intelligence service following outbreak of war. Traveled extensively in the Pacific war areas. Earlier months of 1942 spent in Hollywood writing dialogue for film version of *Pulham.*

1942 *Last Laugh, Mr. Moto.* Mr. Moto went into retirement until revival in the postwar years. Timothy Fuller Marquand born.

1943 *So Little Time,* Marquand's first very best seller and the first of his war novels. Elon Huntington Hooker Marquand born.

1944 Successful adaptation of *The Late George Apley* for the theatre by Marquand and George F. Kaufman.

1945 *Repent in Haste,* second volume in the war "trilogy."

1946 *B. F.'s Daughter* (*Polly Fulton* in English edition), final novel in the war "trilogy."

1949 *Point of No Return,* Marquand's novel of the immediate postwar period.

1951 *Melville Goodwin, U.S.A.* With Paul Osborne adapted *Point of No Return* for a successful Broadway run.

1952 Marquand is "profiled" in *The New Yorker* by Philip Hamburger.

1954 *Thirty Years,* a collection of short fiction and nonfiction with introductory comments and reflections upon his craft by the author.

1955 *Sincerely, Willis Wayde,* Marquand's generally unsympathetic novel of the new American businessman.

1956 *North of Grand Central,* an omnibus collection of the first three New England novels with an introduction by Kenneth Roberts and notes for each by Marquand.

1957 *Stopover: Tokyo,* the last of the Mr. Moto adventures. *Life at Happy Knoll,* a collection of connected short pieces which first appeared in *Sports Illustrated.*

1958 Divorce from Adelaide Hooker Marquand in Nevada. At Carson City he declared that, if he were thirty years younger, he would go West and find materials for his novels in the Nevada area. Remarried following his divorce. *Women and Thomas Harrow,* the last and, in many ways, the most autobiographically interesting of his novels.

1960　*Timothy Dexter, Revisited,* a rewriting of his earlier 1925 historical study of this New England eccentric. Every significant novelist should leave behind him such a revealing book. *Timothy Dexter, Revisited* must be evaluated separately from Marquand's other books since it is a really admirable re-creation of a past era, but it tells much about the novels of the Marquand who could not ultimately reconcile past and present.

Marquand died in his sleep at his home in Newburyport, Massachusetts, July 16, 1960.

John P. Marquand

CHAPTER 1

Mr. Marquand, the Critics,
and the Tradition

I *Voice of an Era*

THE POET KEATS once wrote of Wordsworth in a letter to a friend: "We find what he says true as far as we have experienced, and we can judge no further but by a larger experience—for axioms in philosophy are not axioms until they are proved upon our pulses. We read fine things, but never feel them to the full until we have gone the same steps of the author." Whatever posterity's judgment of the work of John Phillips Marquand may be, there is no question that today his popularity with his readers—his sales run into millions—is the result of a great many men (and women) having "gone the same steps as the author." Just as certainly, Marquand has been the historian of those sociological changes of an age which has seen the organization men of the modern forms of corporate industry challenge the dominance of the family trust in American industrial life and, as a consequence, the class and status relationships of American society. Marquand speaks for his age with an authority which probably no other contemporary writer possesses, not to affirm the values of a mass culture and the organization man, but to challenge such values and to affirm the importance of individual integrity with which the members of that society may resist the increasing vulgarization of American life. His protest is the verbal scalpel with which he cuts away desensitized layers of feeling and then proceeds, with wit and satire, to provide the reader with a confrontation of himself and the standards of his era.

Some time ago Irving Howe presented a definition of mass society which serves admirably to define the subject of John P. Marquand's fiction. Though Mr. Howe intended it to define the social situation confronting the younger novelists of the postwar world who no longer recognize familiar cultural landmarks ("elusive as the moral imperatives of the nineteenth century seemed to novelists of fifty years ago"), his words are as applicable to Marquand's concern during the final twenty years of his career as they are to novelists of a later generation. Mass society, then, Howe defines as a ". . . relatively comfortable, half welfare and half garrison society in which the population grows passive, indifferent and atomized; in which traditional loyalties, ties and associations become lax or dissolve entirely; in which coherent publics based on definite interests and opinions gradually fall apart; and in which man becomes a consumer, himself mass-produced like the products, diversions and values that he absorbs."[1] It is unlikely that Mr. Howe considered Marquand in formulating his definition, but it fits so precisely the developing concerns of the novelist's subject matter—from *The Late George Apley* (1937) to *Women and Thomas Harrow* (1958)—that it may be quoted in this study with the greatest pertinence. The earlier serious novels, beginning with *Apley* and continuing through the writing of *H. M. Pulham, Esquire*, develop the theme of the challenge to traditional loyalties.

During the war years and those immediately following, Marquand's novels continue to contrast the past values of rural and village life with urban and suburban living while at the same time increasing the emphasis upon the vulgarization of the present consumer-centered economy. When we have finished the reading of Marquand's final novel, *Women and Thomas Harrow*, we begin to realize that the novelist has pictured a contemporary world in which traditional associations can be recollected, if at all, only as a kind of sentimental nostalgia without binding principles. It is a world in which chrome-plated vulgarity and unprincipled meanness of spirit have come close to overwhelming any possible traditional loyalties and values, and to destroying in the individual any remaining small hard core of integrity kept alive by a sense of historical perspective.

Marquand tells us much about the manners and the social patterns of post-World War II American life and, first and last, he provides a moral judgment of the quality of that life. His characters again and again are caught up in the demanding though depersonalized mass society, of industry or the arts or communications; and they struggle for material success and security while simultaneously engaged in the effort to discover and to maintain their personal identity. They seek to recover the past as a guide for the present, even though the quest may, and usually does, prove futile. It is a past which provides the perspective and the implicit judgment upon the present, the basis for evaluation of the road taken into the contemporary world, even while it is recognized by the Marquand characters that the road not traveled by cannot in present time be retraced.

We might paraphrase a number of the traits or symptoms of the mass society as outlined by Irving Howe in the development of his definition and discover that they are entirely applicable to the fictional themes of John P. Marquand. Howe recognizes, for example, that social classes continue to exist in mass society, though the divisions are more fluid, less clearly fixed than in earlier decades. Or as Mr. Howe says, "the tokens of class are less obvious." George Apley, finally, had no doubt of the firmness of the barriers of class; Harry Pulham was less sure; Jeffrey Wilson of *So Little Time* and Charles Grey of *Point of No Return* were never quite sure of their status; Willis Wayde comes to realize that he can never belong to one world, the world of tradition and an established culture, and settles for another, the paler imitation world of the organization man.

The earlier novels of Marquand see the family representing a center of authority, binding the individual to apparently changeless values. With increasing freedom from the authority of family, the characters of the later novels find that freedom an increasing burden. Increasingly, too, Marquand's protagonists become ever more aware of life as drift, with the significance of shared experience almost lost to them. His representatives of the mass media, his journalists and news commentators and editorial pundits, increasingly represent the blind leading the blind. Serious controversy is stifled. There are no longer causes which enlist the support or passion of men of conscience, for there is little passion: men like Charles Grey of *Point of No Return* must carefully veil their eyes and stifle the expression of opinion which might suggest nonconformity if they are to achieve the promised land of a vice-presidency. Business increases but significant experience declines. But as material need decreases, there is no joy, no resultant enrichment of life; and the Charles Greys, arrived at the point of no return, wonder whether it was worth it after all. The conclusion: probably not.

Mr. Howe cites the statement of film critic Stanley Kauffman, that the contemporary writer seeks, without finding, great emotional issues which are capable of moving him profoundly. Many younger writers have deliberately chosen to ignore the urban and suburban world of the present as possible subject matter; instead, they "go abroad, go into the past, or go into those few pockets of elemental emotional life left in this country." Marquand both went abroad and into the past, but his basic material continued to be that which, we are told, fails to provide today the intensities of feeling the writer desires. It is no doubt true that "the anguish of the advertising executive struggling to keep his job is anguish indeed, but its possibilities in art are not large-scale."[2] However, large-scale or not, Marquand's treatment of the theme is thorough and searching. His advertising executives, his bank vice-presidents, his business management executives, his professional craftsmen in the arts—all of whom figure in his fictional studies of modern urban and suburban life—share a sense of alienation from, even as they participate in, the American world of the mid-twentieth century. And with varying degrees of concern they are all engaged in what Mr. Howe calls "the recurrent search— in America, almost a national obsession— for personal identity and freedom."

Marquand's subjects, moreover, are those of every major twentieth-century novelist: the frustration of ambition, or the misdirection of that ambition into channels of activity which fail to reward the spiritually misdirected protagonist with the rewards he had sought; or the decline of a standard of gentility which leaves the defenseless protagonist between two worlds. His is the necessity of accepting either the new one and losing the values by which he was reared or the old one with the knowledge that he has subscribed to a set of values which no longer have pertinence in the world of which he is a part; or he discovers that the culture he has accepted is false and cheaply deceptive and that there is no way out if he is to play the game to the end, the rules of which he has accepted at the beginning.

II The Critics

If the critics have given Marquand less than his due (and his achievement may not finally be appraised before a number of years have passed), he at least pretended during his lifetime that it was a matter of no concern to him. Philip Hamburger, in a series of articles appearing some years ago in *The New Yorker* and published later in book form as *J. P. Marquand, Esquire*, has been to date the only writer to evaluate some aspects of his work in terms of biography. Hamburger's "Profile," however, made no attempt to review the individual novels or to pass judgment upon the nature of Marquand's contribution. But Hamburger provides some significant clues to the man—and the work—when he writes that Marquand declared, "I don't know anybody who's had a kind word to say for me since I was a small boy."[3] He asserts, moreover, that Marquand was not disturbed about critical approval or disapproval. He thought of himself, almost certainly, as a professional craftsman who had learned his trade over a long, successful period of apprenticeship, beginning in the early 1920's and ending only in 1936, when he wrote the first of his serious novels, *The Late George Apley*.

But of course in one sense Marquand carried a heavy burden of artistic guilt. For he first achieved limited fame and success through his stories appearing in the mass-circulation magazines. His first work, a novel submitted to the *Ladies' Home Journal*, was sold for a respectable sum; and he continued to sell, without rejections, to such periodicals. It was only after an apprenticeship of some fifteen years in the popular, slick-paper journals that he wrote the novels which gained for him any measure of critical approbation. He is the author of the Mr. Moto stories as well as the creator of George Apley, H. M. Pulham, Jim Calder, Charles Grey, and Melville Goodwin.

Perhaps the critics have been less than kind to Marquand because of this apprenticeship, and yet the Moto stories are deserving of respect. The pervasive themes of Marquand, revealed over and over in the major novels, are implied constantly in his popular fiction. It is puzzling why Marquand should be condemned as a popular writer, or as one who wrote for the mass-circulation magazines, when he has such a respectable body of serious fiction to his credit. Perhaps he should have taken himself somewhat more seriously and labeled his work in a lighter vein "entertainments"—as did Graham Greene. Certainly the serious overtones are present in the Marquand "slick" pieces, just as they are in Greene's popular fiction. Whatever else he may be, Marquand is the novelist of modern marriage in America in the Protestant and Puritan tradition; Greene, also a novelist of marriage, projects the greater metaphysical concern of the individual for his own salvation apart from the binding ties of the social order. Charles A. Brady, one of the Marquand critics to write with admirable discernment, refers to his subject as a

"Martini-Age Victorian." He selected most appropriately the lines from Eliot's *The Cocktail Party* as an epigraph for his essay on the work of Marquand; they express essentially the central theme of disenchantment in these novels of the marital relationship:

> The best of a bad job is all any of us make of it—
> Except, of course, the saints . . .
> . . . contented with the morning that separates
> And with the evening that brings together
> For casual talk before the fire
> Two people who know they do not understand each other,
> Breed children whom they do not understand
> And who will never understand them.[4]

Professor Brady, writing as a Catholic in a Catholic appraisal of the last fifty years of the American novel, sees quite clearly the tradition to which Marquand belongs: the central tradition represented by Fielding, Jane Austen, Thackeray and Trollope, as opposed to that of Laurence Sterne, Emily Brontë, and Graham Greene. "This innate, fastidious Puritanism," he writes, "is, very possibly, the most significant critical fact that can be adduced in Marquand's regard; and, of all his critics, only Stephen Vincent Benét, who was an old hand, anyway, at telling a Puritan hawk from a Cavalier handsaw, had the acumen to note it. . . . His cocktail parties are full of Apleys *agonistes*."[5]

His protagonists are ever aware of "Time's wingèd chariot." His Harry Pulham of *H. M. Pulham, Esquire*, is the essential Marquand character for whom duty and a habit of years come to represent, finally, the ultimate meaning of marriage. And, since like most of the major Marquand characters, boy never gets girl in real life—or not the girl that he believed he wanted—the girl Pulham did not get is finally discovered to be as remote as the moon. Marquand considers repeatedly the agonizing question of the choice once made, or the Frostian road not traveled by. In the novels of Marquand there is always the "Compensation" of the Puritan New Englander, Emerson. Something of the Emersonian conscience survives; the inner voice, whether of God or the Devil, speaks and determines the course to take. Harry Pulham finally decided, as, no doubt had Marquand himself, that he had lived, on the whole, "the only sort of life for which I was really fitted. Perhaps there is some needle inside everyone which points the way he is to go without his knowing it." The road once taken finally becomes so well worn and so familiar that there is only vanity in any attempt to retrace one's steps and thus to recapture a past which is never quite real or substantial. The old lost passion, the endless measuring of the old regret—all is an ultimate futility, and the voice of Ecclesiastes intones its *vanitas vanitatum*. "I could not have gone back if I had wanted to," Harry declares, "because Kay and I had been so long together, and perhaps that was what love really was—not passion or wish, but days and years—and now I was going home." Kay, too, discovers that one can't go back. She tells Harry it's funny. And when he questions her, her reply is the echo of his own thoughts. It's funny "how you have to keep going on," she said, "and how you can't go back." They recognize the sad inevitability of it, as do the characters in Edith Wharton's *The Age of Innocence*.

A thoughtful word has been supplied for the critics by Professor Brady, with which a sympathetic reader of Marquand would find it hard not to agree:

> The representative novel of the eighteenth century had concerned itself with the foundling who found he was an heir; that of the nineteenth with the young man from the provinces who found his way to fortune. The typical novel of the twentieth century has dealt, rather, with life's shattering the youth of sensibility; taken all in all, it might be described as a portrait of the artist *manqué*. Its theme, in a word, is "lost," not "found." Marquand's sophisticated ringing of the changes, in however minor a key, on the centuries' -old, fairytale chord of "found" has hardly endeared himself to the *avant garde* critic.[6]

The sympathetic reader would find it hard to disagree in large part, unless, of course, he had read farther than had Professor Brady at the time he wrote his essay. For it is not at all clear in the last novels of Marquand that the "fairytale chord of 'found'" rings out as clearly as Professor Brady would have us believe—and the reasons for our doubt will be developed more fully in the final chapters of this study. Marquand's own tentativeness of judgment upon his age has perhaps been responsible for the troubled, inconclusive verdicts upon the novels which his more critical readers have expressed.

Among these is the opinion of Nathan Glick that Marquand has been, next to Arthur Koestler, the most "seismographic of contemporary authors." Whereas Koestler, he declares, responds to "cosmic political tremors," Marquand "records the social and cultural flutters of everyday life." And Glick expresses what we may assume to be regret when he writes that Marquand is "alas, our most accomplished novelist of manners." The regret is that the novelist was not a Proust. For Mr. Glick, one of Marquand's best novels, *Pulham,* is little more than a "contemporary footnote to *The Late George Apley.*"[7]

W. J. Smith, writing two years before Marquand's death in 1960, pays tribute to the professional skills of a master craftsman. Marquand, he writes, "offers something rare and wonderful, the charm of craftsmanship, of squared corners and solid oak and careful joinings, of an eye for proportion and an unpretentious decoration, of sensible comforts and sedate humor. Mr. Marquand builds a house that may fall into disfavor, but it will stand sturdy."[8] It would be well if we were to remember the point which Smith makes when finding fault with the Marquand themes, as a number of critics have done. As have other critics before him, Mr. Smith recognizes the difficulty of creating a novel of manners in America and suggests Marquand's problem as a social novelist: the novel of manners in America has been largely undeveloped, despite the best efforts of those who have attempted to practice the genre, because of an aggressive democracy's contempt for the past.

But there is in American life and letters a need for a novel of manners, despite the difficulties of realizing that need, and as Mr. Glick asserts, "It is Marquand's recognition of the changing market for manners and his sensitivity to their quality that sets him apart from all our other social novelists."[9] The novel and the film, he indicates, are now, and have been, the best guides to modes of conduct in our society, owing to the atomization of modern suburban life. And one of Marquand's best novels, *Point of No Return,* is, Glick asserts, the "best fictional source of cultural detail since the early works of Sinclair Lewis." It is interesting to note, incidentally, that Marquand himself once declared (the point is made in Mark Shorer's recent definitive biography of Sinclair Lewis): "I would hesitate to rank myself with Lewis; I don't think I have nearly the same stature. But I am working in his vineyard." Marquand, however, always underestimated his gift, at least publicly. This was equally true of the characters of his novels who, as Mr. Glick observes, were always playing themselves down.

But we may question Glick's conclusion that, while Marquand

is neither a Henry Adams "sounding the return to a purer age" nor a Henry James "struggling for a truer sensibility," he was the bridge between the *Atlantic Monthly* and the *Saturday Evening Post*, "outfitting the new middle classes, whose success values he accepted, with the rusty armor of the aristocracy."[10] The latter half of the statement means little in an interpretation of Marquand's work, for whether he accepted the middle-class values in life or not, he certainly finds them less than a total solution in his fiction. But, then, perhaps we should look beyond the metaphoric coloring of the statement and assert simply that Marquand realized how rusty and unusable was that armor of the "aristocracy" and that he never anywhere assumes that anyone can be clothed with any kind of rusty armor if one wishes to survive in a world that he can, at best, only imperfectly understand.

Leo Gurko, writing in the *American Scholar*, raises a point against Marquand that is difficult for the faithful reader of his novels to refute. Mr. Gurko speaks of the "High Level Formula of J. P. Marquand"—a not unfamiliar charge that Marquand rewrote the same novel a dozen times. The characters in the Marquand gallery reappear in volume after volume. After a listing of the many and obvious virtues of the work of Marquand, whom Gurko accepts as a serious novelist, he charges that the novels are "almost exactly alike. They deal with a fixed problem, and pass through identical stages in the course of working it out. Marquand's technical skill conceals this fact for a time, creating the illusion of variety and change. But when it becomes plain, one realizes that here is the restricting element that has kept Marquand—and will probably always keep him—from reaching the level of his great predecessors."[11] This serious charge cannot be lightly dismissed. It is certainly true that the names of characters fade from mind, not because they are not distinct in the individual novel in which they appear, but because they serve to dramatize a continuing problem with which the novelist himself is involved; and the problem, perhaps, was regarded by Marquand as more serious than the fates of the individual characters.

Probably Mr. Gurko himself supplies the answer and the explanation to the problem of Marquand's novels which he raises. Marquand, he truly asserts, has broken down the barriers between fiction and life: he has made his readers feel that they see in his books their own contemporary uncertainties and doubt of themselves and of our civilization. "The pragmatic cast of Marquand's reflections on larger issues exercises a strong attraction upon his readers" is the way in which Mr. Gurko puts it. And he concludes that Marquand is "bound to a formula, a high-level formula in every sense, but with the rigid limits the word implies."[12]

It will be apparent as we review the novels individually that a whole series of Marquand characters come to remarkably similar conclusions and that certain common themes recur—all referring finally to the central recognition of the vanity of human wishes. His characters realize that one can't have everything and, in the end, are resigned to the necessity of taking less. "The ache of this yielding," states Mr. Gurko "is confined—though never eliminated—by the discovery of [one's] real self. Even to the earlier characters, this growth of self-knowledge is the reward for giving up the achievement of everything."[13]

But in the total view of Marquand's serious fiction it becomes obvious that Marquand simply has no formula, "high-level" or otherwise, as the term is commonly understood, even though it may be easy enough to assume that such was the case in view of Marquand's long apprenticeship in mass-circulation magazines. What looks like formula is really more precisely a kind of compulsion which grows from a personal need to refigure the same sum again and again (and by "sum" we mean a highly personal reading of life), always with the eternally undying hope that eventually a different result may be achieved. What looks like formula is, again, more properly a stubborn reiteration of convictions and principles that are continually reasserted. If the restatement of Kafka's compulsion in his work is a formula, then so is Marquand's. The real point is that Marquand, like any other moralist or like any novelist with a particular view of life, should not be judged adversely because he restates in succeeding novels his basic convictions and beliefs or his ideas, but because these ideas in themselves are limited.

We should never overlook the obvious sense of compulsion in the recurrence of theme and situation in novel after novel. As Mr. Gurko does not, Randall Jarrell apparently recognizes this point and sees the restatement of themes as a reflection, and manifestation, of Marquand's own emotional involvement with the problems which his novels explore. Jarrell acknowledges that Marquand is a very good reporter of his society, but a reporter with very bad troubles. And he declares that "the fiction has underneath it a personal compulsion—that of a wish-fantasy, a day-dream, a nightmare. . . ."[14]

Jarrell further refers to Marquand as one who, though short on talent, imagination, and sheer "brute ability," exercises great care and is long on precise observation and "directed curiosity," but longest of all on "personal involvement, subjective compulsion." When Jarrell writes of Marquand's tendency to present ever new versions of the same subjective fable, he is not saying that a formula is being followed but rather that, as I have suggested, a subjective compulsion brings him back again and again to the theme which Jarrell has parodied in these words: "You were right to do as you did; or if not right, still, you had no choice; or if you had a choice, still, it's the choice all of us necessarily makes wrong: life's life. If only—but it doesn't matter. And . . . it was all so long ago."[15] One may object, as Jarrell does in passing, that the continual flash-backs and the pervasive elegiac mood result in the hero's never having to make, finally, "a clear choice to kiss or kill—the choices are always obscured by the haze of the past, of rueful and lyric recollection."[16]

No doubt what really bothers Mr. Gurko is the conservatism of Marquand's technique. For it is true enough that, from beginning to end of his serious career as a novelist, he used only one technical device, the projecting of past against present by means of the flash-back, and he apparently never felt the need to experiment in devising means of telling his story more effectively. As Alfred Kazin has already made clear, "No matter how much one may admire Marquand's social skill, his wit, his sense of tact, above all his cool honesty, one knows that a Marquand novel will sag into flashback as surely as a Shakespearean hero will spout blank verse." He also suggests, quite properly I believe, that Marquand sometimes, and increasingly toward the end of his career, did not attempt to find "a very convincing or dramatically interesting frame for these flights into the past."[17] The reason may be, as I suppose, that the past became for him increasingly unattainable as a measure and a criterion for the present.

John P. Marquand's own attitude toward his work was certainly critical enough, though he obviously had little use for criticism as such. In a lecture he once delivered at the University of Vermont he declared: "I am a writer, not a critic, and criticism and creative writing are literary oil and vinegar."[18]

Nonetheless, it is obvious enough that he had learned well the lessons of his craft, and I tend to agree with the view of his friend Clifton Fadiman who aptly wrote that "Marquand's whole writing career may be thought of as a series of enlargements. Each of these enlargements stops short of complete escape. Thus the hallmark of his art is the tension resulting from the play between his precise memory of a smaller experience and his growing understanding of a larger one."[19] Without necessarily discovering an ascending order of merit in the successive novels, we do become aware of the fact that each novel represents to a considerable degree an "enlargement," a further step in the developing talent of the age's most remarkable social novelist, an increase in understanding of the individual's relationship to the society and of the meaning of his life.

Despite considerable repetition of themes, of character types, of techniques, there is in his work an evident desire to "'get it right" in the succeeding novel. There is a sense in which he regards each effort as at least a comparative failure, by some final and absolute artistic standard, and his dissatisfaction results in a further effort to attain a perfection which— he must have realized as well as anyone—was, finally, unattainable. For example, thorough reading of Marquand's work from beginning to end of his career reveals his continuing interest in certain types of characters. Army generals seemed particularly to fascinate him. He himself comments in a note regarding a short story of 1926, "Good Morning, Major," that he had apparently presented an inordinate number of generals in the collection of short pieces collected in 1954 as *Thirty Years*. "The truth is that, like most of my contemporaries, I have seen more of generals in my lifetime than I may have wished, and they have always fascinated me as social specimens." Marquand saw, and commented upon, the lack of roundness in the characterization of the officer. But he recognized too, in retrospect, the way in which the time through which we have lived had been responsible for the creation of a more believable military man than those presented satirically in the era between wars.

The repetition, then, so far as his treatment of character types in concerned, was always undertaken with a view to correcting the partial impression, of filling out the picture. The result, as demonstrated in the best novel of an officer in service to appear in our time, is simply justified with *Melville Goodwin, U.S.A.* We also note here Marquand's own recognition of a recurrent pattern in all the novels—the dialectical conflict between the changing world and a set of constant values.

Certainly, the "enlargements" are there in Marquand's novels. His last novel, *Women and Thomas Harrow,* presents a quality of perception that transcends that of the earlier novels, without necessarily being a greater achievement in itself. When we know all of Marquand's novels and place them in their chronological relationship, we discover the steady growth in understanding, even in wisdom, though, as will be pointed out more fully in the final chapter relating to *Thomas Harrow,* that understanding results in a kind of despairing admission of failure in using his art as a means of imposing a set of constant values from the past upon the changing and disorganized world of the present.

The critics have not always seen development in Marquand's novels, even while granting that he served as a weathervane of social change. They have been almost too ready to concur in the confession of Jim Calder, Marquand's protagonist and alter ego in the novel *Wickford Point*: "I had always wanted to do something better, but never had, and probably never would. All I could say for myself at best was that I could keep my place in my field as a technical craftsman if not as an artist, and, as a craftsman, that I could meet its competition." Of course, Marquand became something more than the craftsman that Jim Calder knew himself to be, but he was a skilled story-teller for many years before he was taken seriously, or perhaps took himself seriously, with his Pulitzer Prize winner *The Late George Apley.*

On his part, Marquand was never quite happy about his treatment by the critics; about the credit for achievement withheld; about his omission, for example, from consideration by serious students of contemporary American literature and, in particular, from the text and the individual bibliographies of the *Literary History of the United States.* That, however, was an omission which Professor Robert E. Spiller and his co-editors would have to explain, not Marquand. Still, it was a sensitive point with him, for, as he said, or had Jim Calder say, in *Wickford Point,* "the fiction one writes is so essentially a part of one's ego that disparagement of it is worse than physical pain. Even after years of training one sometimes loses one's self-control."

And no doubt Marquand saw all the compilers of literary histories as stuffy little academic pundits, academicians, "pampered, preposterous creatures who lived an artificial life," as he wrote of the sociologist in *Point of No Return*, "who did not want to understand or be like other people." Like Professor Spiller, they could not write a novel which several hundred thousand people would read, yet they could assign the artist to the proper circle of the Dantean Inferno without granting him a second hearing. "This person is second or third rate," the word went out. "Keep him out of the paradise of the first-class citizen of our ideal literary commonwealth." Marquand's reaction, feeling himself excluded from the Republic of Letters, could not have been other than it was. He once asserted: "I have never understood why a sinner is not allowed at least to attempt reformation in the American World of Letters."

As we review the novels in the pages which follow, I trust that we may concur in an agreement upon an honorable citizenship for John Phillips Marquand in that Republic which he always sought to serve so faithfully.

CHAPTER 2

"Will I ever walk up any road alone?"

CLIFTON FADIMAN once wrote of Marquand: "He is the sympathetic dramatizer of that moment of doubt—the doubt as to whether outer and inner security necessarily coincide—which, though it comes to all of us, is the particular gadfly of the gentility."[1] This observation has particular pertinence when it is applied to the case of George Apley, the protagonist of Marquand's best-known, Pulitzer Prize novel.

"I wish there weren't quite so many new ideas. Where do they all come from?" Such is the pathetic observation George Apley makes to his son in his last years when he finds the modern world beginning to creep into his life. His worry about his daughter's reading of a man named Freud (whom he too reads but only, of course, to discover what his child is thinking) creates for him one of those moments of doubt regarding the coincidence of outer and inner security which he strives to thrust from him. And Horatio Willing, the fictitious narrator of this novel in the form of a memoir,[2] expresses confidently an assurance which George Apley never really felt: "It is a satisfaction to see that we are at a turning of the ways, where the path bends back toward the security of the formulae for which George Apley and the rest of us have stood."

Alas for the George Apleys and the tradition they represented, something more than the firm expression of a wish was necessary to halt the encroachment of modern ideas upon their way of life. Of course, as Apley wrote his son John in New York, he had heard about Cubism before the war and had "laughed as heartily as anyone at the Nude Descending the Staircase, but now to see supposedly intelligent people gaping at a wall full of paint slobbered willy-nilly over canvas makes me feel that the world is going mad." For George Apley the Monets at the art museum were quite radical enough.

I *Atomization of Society*

The Late George Apley, Marquand's first major contribution to the modern *comédie humaine* which he was engaged in writing during the final twenty-five years of his life, has received widespread recognition and perhaps the firmest approval by critics of all his work. Indeed, even in 1941 Joseph Warren Beach found it possible to declare, on the basis of only two of Marquand's New England novels which had appeared to that time, that *Apley* was likely to be remembered as "the prime example of Marquand's art." And he could assert further that Marquand's reputation was so well established with critics and discerning readers that, "if he has anything else to say, he will be sure to get a hearing . . . but what he has said already is arresting enough to give him a very respectable rank in American letters."[3]

Of course, as subsequent chapters will attempt to establish, Marquand had a great deal more to say. *The Late George Apley* can certainly be read appreciatively without reference to the later books, but it must be said that, without a knowledge of that *something more* which Marquand contributed to his interpretation of the modern world, an additional dimension necessary for full understanding is missing from *Apley.*

At the risk of oversimplification we may define Marquand's work from *The Late George Apley* (1937) to *Women and Thomas Harrow* (1960) as being concerned with the increasing atomization of contemporary society. The point of the first novel is that the community dominates the individual; imposing a certain social conformity, it insures at the same time a constant set of social references and a measure of security. The later novels present individuals increasingly adrift in a society without values or, more accurately, a society largely indifferent to humanistic values since the standards of the corporate business and industrial structure have been substituted for them. His characters reflect the need of the urbanized modern man for a community relationship in which he may give as well as get, in which he may serve as well as be served. As we shall presently see in a detailed examination of *The Late George Apley,* one virtue of the Apley world is its retention of the Calvinistic principle of responsible stewardship. It is a significant point which not all critics have been aware of, any more than have many modern readers. Joseph Warren Beach, for example, was most unfair, although perhaps for understandable reasons, when he wrote of George Apley that

"Giving away money was one way of extending one's power and declaring one's virtue." Certainly the Apley men, reared through the generations in the conviction that privileges imposed duties and obligations, would have been thoroughly shocked and offended by such an interpretation of their motives.

Of course, to say so much does not at all imply that Marquand himself whole-heartedly approved of Apley's world. The novel, after all, has a satirical edge. And he makes it quite clear that there is often a narrow margin between moral principle and pharisaical self-righteousness. But if he does not approve entirely of this past New England order, neither does he find the world of modern corporate finance of Charles Grey in *Point of No Return* fully satisfactory. The unachieved, perhaps unachievable, ideal requires a nice balance between the individual and a stable, principled, on-going community evolving from tradition.

From beginning to end, Marquand never ceases to insist upon the essential humanistic values. George Apley, like Thomas Harrow, was essentially a decent, honorable, morally principled person who defended the worth and dignity of the individual and the humanistic tradition of which he was a part. Harrow, to be sure, is much more fully aware of the degradation of the democratic ideal in modern America than was Apley, the representative of an earlier generation; but though confused and lost in a world now but imperfectly understood, he continued to insist in his own life upon the validity of those values upon which the American nation was founded. All of the characters in the later novels strive to achieve in life a purposeful relationship with others, even while realizing the steadily declining possibilities for meaningful relationships. George Apley values increasingly the fact of the existing relationship with the community of which he is a part, even though he often questions its purposefulness.

The question, or one of the questions, raised in *Apley* is whether the individual can remain a member of an organic community without crippling his individual nature through a complete submission to conformity. The novel shows the young George Apley engaging in a number of rather weak attempts at revolt against an imposed conformism. Eventually, however, upon the death of his father, he assumes his obligations to the family and the community and submits to the disciplines which his position imposes upon him. Apley once said of himself: "I am the sort of man I am, because environment prevented my being anything else." Of course, this conviction was apparently shared by Marquand, since virtually all of his characters accord the same essential significance to the influence of environmental factors. The real point, however, is that the statement implies a rather precise knowledge of "the sort of man I am," and nothing could have been farther from the truth in the case of Marquand's protagonists. The central irony of his novels lies in his characters' failure to realize aspects of their own natures which are nonetheless apparent enough to the reader. Still, eventual self-knowledge is the final and greatest reward for a life which has failed to realize the full measure of its youthful aspiration.

II *New England Values*

George Apley, the descendant of a family which first planted its roots in Massachusetts early in the seventeenth century, was born in 1866 and died in 1933. Thus his lifetime covered a period marked by unprecedented change and development. Throughout his life he never failed to read his Emerson and to make the usual pious observances honoring past New England worthies who had belonged to an agrarian world rapidly giving way to a strange new industrial order. The Apleys had been manufacturers, bankers, lawyers, merchants, respectable pillars of society and Harvard men for generations. They had amassed fortunes which, kept intact, were passed down to succeeding generations. In George Apley's time the principal source of family income was the Apley Textile Mills, capably managed by Uncle William Apley. A man of the most unquestioned probity, he was nonetheless a vigorously relentless competitor who realized that George, then a boy, lacked the firmness and the business acumen to carry on the family enterprise, a conviction which George's father, Thomas Apley, came to share. George seemed lacking in those qualities of Yankee shrewdness which had built and preserved the Apley fortune. His father persuaded him to become a lawyer since, it seemed probable, he might by character and training be able to manage the estates of others conservatively and well whereas his own property might be unwisely dissipated. It was for that reason that Thomas Apley set up a trust fund to assure the continuance of the Apley fortune and the family security.

But if George Apley failed to inherit business acumen (though as an investor he was prudent enough), he did have passed on to him the New England faith in high thinking and plain living.

The Apleys always avoided any obvious show of ostentation. Their frugality without meanness set them apart as possessors of "old money." Though George Apley's two children found something humorous in their Great-uncle William, their father admonished them for their amusement. "The only thing that surprises me is your belief that he should change," he wrote, "when his care in living is a part of his philanthropy. From the time of the Roman Empire down, indulgence in the externals of wealth has never benefited a community. Your uncle realizes that there are more important things than modern plumbing; I pray that you two will come to that realization in time."

George Apley had himself been similarly admonished as a child and been made to understand the value of money. As his father had once written him, "MY DEAR LITTLE MAN: Here is your ten-cent piece and do not forget that this is a good deal of money. Think of it this way: it can buy ten lead pencils or two tops and a string, or enough candy to make you very ill. Please try to think carefully exactly what you want, before you spend it, because there is no satisfaction as great as spending wisely, and few annoyances as great as feeling that money has been wasted. . . ."

George Apley, in writing to his children about their great-grandfather Moses Apley, one of the richest shipping men in the Boston of an earlier time, points out to them that, while it had been said he was "somewhat relentless in his later dealings, no one has questioned his uprightness or his probity." Indeed, as proof of Moses Apley's charitable instincts, George Apley reminds his young children that it was their great-grandfather's two-hundred-thousand dollar endowment which made possible one of the principal Apley charities, the Apley Sailors' Home.

The charities of the Apleys were many, large sums often being given anonymously. George Apley's father, Thomas, left an estate of staggering proportions, so great indeed that George himself could hardly believe the size of the individual bequests in his will. It had been made possible because, as his father had told him, he had always lived on a small fraction of his income, had retained a similar small proportion for contingencies, and had given the rest to charity. As George Apley in turn confesses to his son, until his father's death "your mother and I were living on an income of ten thousand dollars a year, and this seemed adequate for all our needs." Characteristically, they regarded the greatly increased income as an actual embarrassment.

To understand the Apleys, their pride of family, their New England conscience and their sense of obligation to the community, it is necessary to understand their doctrine of stewardship which emerged from Calvinistic New England and found further secular expressions in the social and ethical principles of Emersonian transcendentalism. George Apley passes it on to his son as he had received the doctrine in turn form his father. George Apley writes:

It has always seemed to me that great establishments are senseless and egotistical and do not help one's name in a community. It is better to think of one's self as a steward who owes the community a definite debt; and such I have always tried to be, as my father was before me.

My father once made a remark which I shall now repeat to you because it illustrates this attitude. One evening not very long before his death, when I was seated with him on the Hillcrest piazza watching the gold of the setting sun on the leaves of the great elms, I happened to make some casual remark about the servants, when my father stopped me by beating on the floor with his walking stick. "I do not like the word 'servants,'" he said, "when it is employed to differentiate a certain class of persons from ourselves. In a sense we all are servants, placed here on earth to serve. Some of us, by the will and the omniscience of the Divinity, have been given a greater task than others; I count myself, somewhat to my sorrow, as a member of that group. It is a very grave thought to me to think that I may soon have to render an account of my stewardship to my Maker. I have held control of some large industries in this country and through them I have controlled the lives of many people. This is a solemn thought and some day it will be a solemn thought for you. There are certain definite obligations for one in my position and one in yours—and one of them is to try to make your life worth while with the advantages God has given you. When one is the steward of a large fortune one should not dissipate it by useless spending.

The sentiment is somewhat archaic in the present day, George Apley admits, but he would be happy to see his son accept his responsibility when his time comes as he himself had always attempted to do.

Old Thomas Apley's firmly held sense of social obligation is no less sincere because he finds it possible to assent to his brother William's harsh measures in the expulsion of certain "agitators" and "subversive groups" (union organizers) from the

Mills. It was quite clear to him, as it should have been to others, that any other course would have been to abdicate a part of the obligation and moral responsibility imposed upon him "by the will and omniscience of the Divinity." We would hesitate to term the creed by which he lived hypocrisy when he subscribed to it as sincerely as he did.

To be sure, the importance of family could prove to be an annoyance which one might find more than a little trying on more than one occasion, particularly in young manhood. George Apley wrote one of his college friends, expressing an intense distaste for the rule of family, the heavy hand of tradition bearing down upon his life. "I have had family dinned in my ears ever since I have been able to think," he confessed. "My life has been governed by the rigours of blue-nosed bigots who have been in their graves for a century. . . ." However, his biographer, Mr. Horatio Willing of Boston, apologizes for this slip on Apley's part, terming it an "erratic change" of mood. Actually, Mr. Willing assures us, the *real* George Apley was thoroughly sound; these erratic opinions were most unrepresentative of the George Apley whom he had known for a lifetime.

III   *A Report of Life*

The egregious Mr. Willing asks himself the question which he rightfully points out as most significant: what is truth in a life? "In order to delineate character there must be an artistic stressing of certain qualities—but are these the vital qualities? Who has the right to say?" Mr. Willing might well ask. While Marquand has great sport with his pompous narrator, he probably would have been the first to agree with the pertinence of Willing's question. We might say that Marquand, in all of his creative years, was attempting to write a biography, a true report of a life. His *Apley,* almost before he got well started, is a recognition of the futility of his project. His final book is almost a redraft of his earlier confession that it is quite impossible to see the full picture of the man, and he suggests in an essay, originally given as a lecture, that interpretations of character in literature or in life depend upon degrees of sensitivity and understanding.

It is a measure of Marquand's skill, his insight, and his accomplishment that he always sought to present as objectively as possible the full-dimensioned character without ever assuming that his portrait would be accepted with equal understanding by all his readers. For example, I find myself forced to disagree strongly with a statement like that of Joseph Warren Beach that George Apley, as head of the family, "had the satisfaction of putting on the screws financially" when he attempted, successfully, to prevent cousin John Apley from divorcing his wife and marrying another woman. My own reading would insist that we see George Apley whole, and whether we might agree or disagree with his decision in the case of cousin John, we should recognize that George Apley followed the only course which his dedicated sense of obligation could permit him to follow. Furthermore, it is utterly false to assume that Apley "enjoyed" applying the screws. But, of course, this is precisely Marquand's point. Men like George Apley, reared in the dedication to a tradition, might, if they were lesser men doing their best and trying to defend a creed by which they had been trained, defend the proper cause for the wrong reasons. They might, in short, fail in imagination and true courage, but, after all, they had to live by the only creed they knew, and George Apley always tried to interpret that creed as ably as his understanding permitted.

The point of the novel, then, is that Apley's son John, a man of Marquand's own generation, has asked his father's friend, Horatio Willing, to write about his father as he truly was, to paint his portrait—as Cromwell said—with all his warts on. Young John Apley, who has finally come back to Boston after his period of revolt to take up the family burden and to assume his father's obligations, asks only that the biographer write the whole truth about George Apley. That truth, he asserts, had not been presented in the tributes spoken over his dead body, and "personally, I think he would like the truth for once. I hope so because I was rather fond of him." Young John Apley recalls that his father was often kind to him, that they used to go camping together, and while they did not really understand one another, that Father always had a façade which one had to break through before understanding could set in. When George Apley was angry with his son and felt that he had somehow been let down, he reminded him—a reminder which the son never forgot—that he was the only father John would ever have and that John was the only son whom he would ever know. Therefore, they should make the best of it. And "let us try not to forget it." John insists that the book be written honestly about his father, for, as he tells Horatio Willing—much to that worthy's displeasure—"You know, and I know, that Father had guts." Mr. Willing never quite got over the indelicacy of that word.

So, what kind of man was George Apley? That is what Horatio Willing (and John P. Marquand, though their answers are obviously somewhat different) sets out to determine. "He had," writes Willing, "the essential, undeviating discipline of background, which the letter of his son gives me the incentive to display."

The Late George Apley is an extraordinarily subtle book since the reader is likely to interpret the character of the memoir in terms of Willing's interpretation; and, as we see Apley through Willing's eyes, we must depend upon our own perceptivity as readers for a truer evaluation than that provided by an unusually insensitive narrator. Marquand himself declared that he had written better than he knew, for readers charged him with the pompous and ungrammatical style and the outright illiteracies of his narrator. "I hope," wrote Marquand more than twenty years after the book appeared, "that the experience has taught me to be more careful."[4]

There was, as Marquand himself admitted, a temptation to resort to slapstick farce, owing to the stances of Willing and Apley which often verge upon the preposterous—a temptation which had to be resisted, since satire should be serious. Marquand's latter-day reflections upon *Apley* continued with the assertion that after finishing the book he realized it was far better than the mediocre serial stories he had been publishing in the popular magazines for years; furthermore, it had been easier to do. (The unconfirmed report that his agent urged him to put it aside since it would never come to anything may or may not be true.) "For almost the first time in my life," he declared, "I had written about something that I thoroughly understood. I had translated something of myself and my own experience into *The Late George Apley,* and I had achieved through my experience an unforseen depth and reality. In fact, I had been able to make an indirect comment on life as I had known it, which indeed may be the only valid reason for writing any novel."[5]

Experience, he knew, had to be there if he was to write significantly. And while he asserted that he did not regard *Apley* as a great success, financially or otherwise, nor as his best novel, its immediate success with readers and critics alike, and its continuing popularity, its successful adaptation for the theatre, are all factors contradicting the judgment of Marquand. He professed to see whatever popularity the book had as being based upon the simplicity and originality of the framework. The epistolary form was certainly venerable enough, but the new addition to the form was his use of the device as a parody and his creation of the egregious Mr. Horace Willing, a character, incidentally, which achieved such vigorous life and such a firm hold upon Marquand's imagination that, as noted in the preface, he permitted himself to be pilloried verbally sometime later by a letter from Mr. Willing to Dr. Huntington of the Boston Tavern Club. The decision to employ parody of the epistolary form was a brilliant stroke, providing as it does a suitable frame for the presentation of the more sensitive Apley against a background of Willing's obtuse interpretations.

Such a passage as that which follows tells us as much of Willing as it does of Apley; it manages to concentrate in a single brief paragraph all of those features of the society which make it most vulnerable to satirical treatment: its self-satisfied complacency, its provincial smugness.

> To those of us who know it and are a part of it there is nothing unnatural in the preoccupation of a Bostonian with his environment; for order—so lamentably lacking in other cities—tends to make him so completely at home and so contented with his social group that he is unhappy in any other. [George Apley struggles against this dreary conclusion but comes, finally, to accept its truth.] Starting with the nucleus of the family and its immediate friends, and next to it the school attended by these same contemporaries, he finally reaches the dancing class, and then the Thursday afternoons, and next the Friday evenings. A young girl will be introduced into society and will join the Sewing Circle of her year; a boy will be taken into his father's Club at Harvard. There is a simplicity in this procedure which emanates, I think, from the laudable similarity of ideas which makes up Boston life. These ideas have their foundation on the firm substratum of common sense which runs back to the beginnings of our colonial founders. This common sense, combined with an appreciation of what is truly fine, has given us a stability and a genuine society in a chaotic, nervous nation. If this society has moulded an individual in conformation to its principles, I, for one, cannot see why this is a deplorable situation, as every human being must conform to the social demands of his group, what ever that group may be. If George Apley failed to meet

certain challenges, let us admit that we all stand together as one large family. Collectively, in habits and ideals, our group is a family group where kinship, however distant, stretches into the oddest corners.

Of course, the pattern is not only that of George Apley's conditioning but also of Henry Pulham's, of *H. M. Pulham, Esquire* in the succeeding generation—just as, it is implied, it was that of George Apley's son John. Willing apparently does not realize how closely the pattern of acculturation approximates similarly motivated rites of the Trobriand Islanders, but Marquand does— as did his anthropologist of *Point of No Return* who visits a New England town, fresh from a study of primitive tribes, to apply the same criteria in his work on *Yankee City.*

The quoted paragraph, a kind of quintessential example of the novel's flavor, does indicate the culture's complacency and its smugness, but there is something else there—at once admirable and pathetic. In a nation which has never fully understood nor accepted the idea of society, Willing's (and Apley's) Boston seems, at one level, an enviable exception. On the other hand, there is something unenviable, and almost pathetic, about a society which chokes off revolt and the potentiality of change or development among its members. This, obviously, is Marquand's point; for while seeing the virtues of an ordered community, he cannot condone the crippling of the individual who must sacrifice all—any hope of happiness—to conformity and a low-level utilitarian greatest-good-for-the-greatest-number concept.

A part of the social responsibility of the Apleys and their kind is to collect something, anything, which may be contributed to the community at the end of one's life. George Apley chooses oriental bronzes, which, though he didn't particularly care for them himself, had been recommended to him by his Uncle William who had been collecting oriental ceramics. But even this commitment of the Apleys, as pointless as it might seem, was probably viewed as not entirely senseless by Marquand, who was a great collector himself and certainly far from free of his New England heritage and the sense of stewardship. Indeed, one may assume that Marquand has written truly of an impulse and a conviction which has ruled most of the second and third generation inheritors of great wealth, by whom most of our major philanthropic foundations today have been endowed.

The Horace Willing statement, which I have quoted at length above, illustrates more than one facet of the Apley—and the Boston—mentality of which Marquand is writing. "Ideas," he writes, "have their foundation on the firm substratum of common sense." And indeed the point is demonstrated over and over again throughout the novel. One Bostonian, Willing tells us, had the promise of a brilliant career, but it has "been clouded by an unbalanced preoccupation over social injustice." Common sense and New England tradition led Thomas Apley, George's father, to ignore for many years that "Popish holiday" of Christmas and to give his gifts at New Year's; these influences, more significantly, led him to observe Thanksgiving Day, before all other holidays, as the "high festival of the year, combining as it did pious thanks for plenty which the year had bestowed and a refurbishing of family ties." Common sense is present in Thomas Apley's adjuration to his son that "nothing is more important than social consideration." Common sense is revealed in Thomas Apley's reminder to his son that he must never forget how much "appearances count in a world of business and credit," and that he must "be careful not to offend"—the examples might be multiplied almost endlessly.

And what was love and marriage like in this well-regulated world into which George Apley finally came to play his part? As a Harvard student, George Apley met, and fell in love with, a girl named Mary Monahan, from the wrong part of Boston and from a class unrelated to that of Apley's background. It was, to be sure, an idealistic, high-minded relationship, though in the opinion of Horatio Willing it was a "youthful lapse," one of which he had to write despite his wish that it might remain buried in the past. "Anyone at a certain stage of life," Willing explains, "may be beset by vagaries which must not be considered seriously."

Almost from the beginning there was no chance for George Apley's happiness. His mother reminded him that he would always be "the gallant knight." Eventually he would marry someone from his own class, someone who, Mother Apley wrote, would be like a character from her "dear Jane Austen," with sense and sensibility. And Mother Apley recommends a member of the clan, "dear Catherine Bosworth," who had been brought up as George Apley had been reared, who shared his interests and his attitudes; for after all, Catherine had been brought up "to know that true happiness in life, such as your dear father and I have shared, is not based on external show."

Mr. Horatio Willing assures us that Miss Monahan "had many of the externals of a young person of a higher position." She almost passed—but not quite. Indeed, when she once walked with George Apley on Commonwealth Avenue, she was even taken by some passers-by for a Baltimore belle. However, it should be understood that Miss Monahan belonged to the encroaching Irish element in the city. To Horatio Willing she was the "Monahan woman," and he declares that "if latitude was offered him [Apley] by the young Monahan woman, . . . he took no advantage of it. This is the one pleasing aspect of an affair which obviously could not be of long duration."

Naturally enough the rumors came to the ears of Thomas Apley and certain results inevitably followed. Young Apley, in a series of letters to Mary Monahan from which Horatio Willing quotes discreetly, protests his love with growing desperation, declaring firmly that when his parents come to know her they will accept her and understand everything. "Once they do," he attempts to reassure her, as well as himself, "you'll find that all the Apleys stick together, and that you will be one of us. . . ." But it was not to be, and we next hear of George Apley's being packed off to Europe for a good long rest. His mother writes him that she had not realized how overtired her dear boy was getting and that, when he returns, he shall not want for "a mother's love, a father's love, or a dear sister's love." Father Apley applies a familiar type of emotional blackmail, telling his son that his mother had been so "unwell that I have been deeply worried about her and I will not have her upset further. You will view matters in quite a different light after a change of scene and will understand your obligations as a member of our family." George Apley was, comments his biographer, "meeting the severe shock which comes to all of us who must reconcile inclination with obligation."

When an Apley traveled he was always discovering how much other places were like Boston. In the determined gayety of his letters home to his mother, whose spiritual cannibalism he never recognizes, he speaks of the similarity of old England to New England, of that of the Champs Elysées to Commonwealth Avenue. He writes more frankly to a contemporary that he and his fellow travelers had seemingly transferred their own culture to every place they visited instead of receiving new impressions of different cultures. But his Uncle Horatio, who has accompanied him, finds nothing unnatural about the fact. ". . . I am quite convinced," he says, "and you will be convinced in time, that our own culture and our own morals are a good deal better and finer than those of the people around here. Find a Bostonian and you will find a citizen of the world." However, George Apley still has his moments of doubt: on one occasion, as he observes a quiet rural road in France, he wishes that he might walk up it to see something for himself "without guidance and without advice." And he asks rather wistfully, "I wonder, will I ever walk up any road alone?"

Following his return there are additional moments of resistance to the conformity which is being imposed upon him. For a short time there are the forbidden pleasures, the moments of levity and conviviality which he finds at the Berkley Club. On such evenings he almost forgets on occasion that he is Thomas Apley's son George. As he wrote a friend, "When half the evening is gone we do not seem to care very much who we are or where we came from. We are able to laugh and talk, quite confident that the walls have no ears to speak of. . . ." But ears or no, Thomas Apley wrote him from New York that while "a certain amount of merriment is all very well, . . . one must be careful of the company which one chooses for such occasions. They must be from your own class." This advice George Apley takes and is later able to pass on to his own son.

Not long afterward Mother Apley's recommendation for an addition to the clan, "dear Catherine Bosworth," prevails. In marriage, above all in marriage, family interests are the primary considerations. Joseph Warren Beach writes of George Apley's, and the family's, choice as being "a good deal of an invalid [who] remained heavily dependent on her parents all her life." It is difficult to understand how she could have been thus termed. If Professor Beach referred to spiritual invalidism, he could not have been far from the point, but certainly Catherine Bosworth Apley was vigorous enough in the physical sense. She had in common with other New Englanders of the class the indomitable will and the whim of iron which permitted the creation of a behind-the-skirts matriarchy. Platitudinously, Mother Bosworth was writing young George Apley that she was not so much losing a daughter as gaining a son, while at the same time Mother Elizabeth Apley was writing Catherine Bosworth that she was not so much losing a son as gaining a daughter—and both meant it, indubitably. It was only a question of which female will would prevail, and the result was almost a fore-gone conclusion—two female wills, mother and daughter, against the one will of the bridegroom's mother. Beach refers to a Boston marriage as "the great sacrifice." And so the sacrament appears to be. Naïvely, Willing declares that many Boston men had been overcome by the occasion and had succumbed or fled in the face of the excitement. He speaks of "several persons with the very best background who have disappeared from Boston on the eve of matrimony," and he asserts that while "most of these have re-established their position at some time later, . . . two, to the writer's certain knowledge, have never been heard of since."

The dominant role of woman in the life of the community is emphasized repeatedly. Marriage in Apley's Boston is not entered into with any conviction on the part of the male that he has triumphed or achieved a conquest. As George Apley later wrote his son: "There is not much place in this world for personal gratification, nor is this particularly becoming to the people in our position." It was a conclusion which one had as well accept since there was really no escape from the situation for "people of our position."

It is not unlikely that Professor Beach was taken in by the word of Mother Bosworth that Catherine was not really very robust and that she is convinced that dear George would never think of taking her too far away from her father and mother. The father of the bride also writes George of his hope and expectation that Catherine will never be taken farther away than suburban limits. George's father writes that "her position and yours in the scheme of things are such that there will be none of the frictions due to divergent backgrounds, which might occur for instance in a New York and Boston union."

Everything has been arranged for the young couple. Thomas Apley has made all the preparations for his son's legal career, for his admission into the best clubs. There is some question regarding their honeymoon trip, but when the matter is finally decided they are permitted only a brief period together; for, as George Apley wrote his long-time friend and biographer Horatio Willing, Catherine's parents had joined them at the Narra-gansett House and Catherine was pleased: . . . "two weeks alone is rather a long time. . . ."

In the years that follow two children are born, a son and a daughter. George attempts to distinguish himself by a historical paper, read at the Boston clubs and later printed privately, on a Boston property which has changed hands numerous times over the years. And, indeed, he does find himself becoming more and more widely accepted as a responsible member of the community. He pursues an endless variety of civic responsibilities, but occasional doubts arise as to what all the activity adds up to. When his father reminds him that he and his group are obligated to carry forward their responsibilities to the community, George finds himself wondering what his life is all about. He sees his father as a giant, capable of shaping public affairs and maintaining the status quo, but he is less confident of himself. As his father puts the matter in blunt terms: "This talk about the common good is arrant Socialism and nonsense. You and I stand for the common good. We stand for a small class, but you don't see it. Thunderation! Nobody sees it but me and my contemporaries. . . . You represent to me the definite end of an era. When control is gone, and it is slipping fast, Boston will become moribund, atrophied; and I for one shall be very glad to leave it."

George Apley had to agree that in one sense he felt his father was right, and he certainly believed that there were no men like Thomas Apley left in Boston. The men who followed after him, he concluded, were only pale reflections, unable to carry the burden of responsibility which they had apparently shouldered so effortlessly. And George Apley, rather sadly, concluded:

> It sometimes seems to me that my father's generation did all there was to do, and left nothing to the rest of us. Thus we have been left in a curious position. Most of us have obeyed the older generation so implicitly that now they are gone there is nothing left but to continue in the pattern they have laid down for us. Or is it that we have not the originality to change that pattern? Or is it that we have not the wish? It may be, like the Chinese, that we are finally ending in a definite and static state of ancestor worship, that the achievements of the past are beyond our present capacities. My father was that past.

Willing sees the statement as an expression by George Apley of one of his more erratic moods. But it is, of course, one of the moments of honesty when Thomas Apley's son questions, even though briefly, the imbalance of his society. Even Thomas Apley, shortly before his death, had his moments of doubt, for almost on his last day he said, "Elizabeth, I have been thinking something. I wonder if it would have been better if George had married that little Irish girl." Of course, Elizabeth concluded after her husband's death that it had been quite apparent to her that poor Thomas had been slipping mentally for some time.

And so George, released "from the belittling task of making money, but not from the responsibility which springs from his freedom," sets out to follow in his father's footsteps. He takes up the life of his father, even though he attempts occasionally to get away from Boston, as when he purchases an island off the coast of Maine to which, at first, only men were invited. In the end, however, the women take over this refuge; in middy blouses, khaki skirts, black cotton stockings and black sneakers, they organize the program for the day, which requires rising at sunrise. Apley writes plaintively that he had hoped to get away for awhile from certain things, for a breath of air out of the Boston atmosphere, but Boston inevitably came to Pequod Island. In one of these Chesterfieldian letters which George Apley cannot refrain from writing his son John he declares: "This is an inescapable fact but one, I believe, that we should be rather proud of than otherwise. It is something to be an integrated part of such a distinct group. It is somehow reassuring; at any rate you can go to Bar Harbor, John, but you cannot get away from Pequod Island." And years later, John Apley appended a note to the letter, saying, "By God, you can't."

Perhaps we see George Apley most clearly in his letters to his son. It is then that he reveals himself most nakedly. He tells the boy who must follow his as a responsible Apley that ". . . a large part of life consists of learning how to be unhappy without worrying too much about it." And when George Apley tried hardest to follow, unsuccessfully, in the footsteps of his father, young John Apley, of Marquand's own generation, concludes that "Dad doesn't mean half he says; half the time he's trying to be somebody else."

Perhaps that is the tragedy of George Apley. Despite the training, and the upbringing, and the values he has been living by, he is never quite sure who he really is. As his son writes, "I have a shrewd suspicion now that Father, much as he tried, had a good deal of difficulty himself in adjusting to his environment. . . . I don't believe he ever liked half of what he did, but simply everlastingly carried on, like the British Army."

The difficulty of adjustment is demonstrated in George Apley's later attempts to balance his privileges by his obligations through his reform efforts. It was George Apley's credo, passed on to his son, that one would spend much of one's life among intelligent people; therefore one should learn to be intelligent. But when Apley attempted to reform Boston and take it away from the Irish political bosses, he found himself compromised and his reputation as an upright individual threatened. It is at this juncture, rather melodramatically, that the former Mary Monahan once more enters his life. Arrested by two policemen in a hotel room with some ladies of questionable reputation, he is saved from public disgrace and the defamation of his family name only by the intervention of the girl he had once loved. Her husband, an influential Irish politician, manages everything; and Apley escapes the trap, after employing the detectives who were used to destroy him, finding them wonderful fellows and apparently being so ingenuous that he never realizes how he has compromised his reform movement.

But to say that he blinds himself to the implications of his position is not to say that he has been a conscious hypocrite. He is, still, what he has always been—the product of his environment. As he writes his son at a later period, "It is only because I see so clearly that a great part of my uneasiness in previous years has been entirely wasted effort. I have been chafing in a way at an environment, and only lately it has been coming over me that it is the only environment in which I could possibly have survived. I am thankful that I am in it. Some day you will be too, John." And one must conclude that probably John was—some day.

Joseph Warren Beach has written:

> The social philosophy of George Apley was that of a man of inherited wealth, whose chief fetish is the conservation of what he has. He was not himself a money-maker nor a contributor to the production of wealth. But he took over almost unmodified the individualistic political economy which suited the great industrialists of the nineteenth century. He relied solely on the judgment of competitive business to correct the evils to which competitive business had given rise. The social measures undertaken under Hoover and Roosevelt were all to him so much socialistic nonsense. His views on the Sacco-Vanzetti case were those of President Lowell.[6]

And so they were. More and more, in the last years of his life, George Apley came to rely upon the views of his father, Thomas Apley, who had pontificated and practiced for an earlier generation in a way that George Apley had never been able to do for his own. His children revolt against him and his standards and values. And they reject his way of life, though John recognizes what his father represented and eventually, after his extended period of revolt, comes home to carry on, even though he has offended the Boston and the Apley canon by marrying a divorcée.

Joseph Warren Beach wrote—a great many years ago, and on the basis of two serious novels—that Marquand was more clever than serious. But if Marquand has one of the more brilliant styles, one of the most convincing treatments of his materials, it is hardly fair to charge him with mere "cleverness" because his dialogue seems more deftly polished and believable than that of most of his contemporaries. Beach believed that Marquand's concern was primarily with intellectual rather than with emotional commitments. The supposition misses the point by a mile. Marquand was more than a little involved in the emotional frustrations of his protagonists, and he certainly saw George Apley as something more than a curious freak. There was a universal quality in George Apley which transcended his Boston birth and rearing, for as Marquand himself wrote:

> Wherever a few generations of leisure combine with inherited security, there will develop a pattern of manners, attitudes, and politenesses. There are Apleys in Paris and London today, and they are no doubt developing in Moscow and Peiping. They will never become, I hope, entirely extinct.[7]

It is a hope in which readers over the years will no doubt concur.

Certainly one of the most affectionate tributes paid the book was that of an anonymous writer in the "Notes and Comment" section of *The New Yorker* shortly after Marquand's death. The book is, declared the writer, "the finest extended parody composed in modern America . . . . a detailed valentine to a city—Boston—such as no other American city can expect to receive. . . ." And, equally significant, it is the "best-wrought fictional monument to the nation's Protestant elite that we know of."[8] The writer indicates that the satire, ferocious yet urbane, manages to leave with us the rather startling conclusion that the Apleys, if no better than other men, are in the final analysis certainly no worse.

An interesting feature of *Apley* is that in the course of the memoir we discover qualities of individuality where we had been led to expect only conformity. George Apley reminds his son upon John's decision to return to Boston that there are certain things one cannot get away from; that, after his fling, he is now quite properly coming home to take up his responsibilities, even though reluctantly. The point is that we have seen the father, and indirectly the son, as individuals before each in turn takes up his membership in the Berkley and the Province clubs, those conformist "havens of refuge where no one wishes to be emotionally disturbed."

As one writer has pointed out, "The typical Marquand hero reaches the point of no return when he draws his first breath."[9] George Apley is no exception, though it was a long time before he could accept the fact of resignation to his destiny of fate and breeding. So one can't go home again? For Apley the road he took, despite detours, always turned toward home.

CHAPTER 3

The Brills of Wickford Point:
A New England Idyl

CURZON'S MILL, north of Newburyport, is the setting for Marquand's second satirical novel of New England manners. He calls it "Wickford Point" and describes it for the reader in loving detail. Eighteen years after the publication of *Wickford Point* in 1939 he published a personal essay in the *Atlantic* titled "Hearsay History of Curzon's Mill" which confirms, if confirmation beyond that provided in the novel were needed, his sentimental attachment to this small region of New England.

Located on the Artichoke River, a tidal stream, the property had been in the possession of Marquand's family since 1820. From childhood on he had heard legends of life at the Mill from his Great-aunt Mary Russell Curzon and Aunt Mary Marquand. It was well known by all the family that Great-aunt Elizabeth Curzon Hoxie had "made beds and washed and served in the Brook farm experiment. . . ."[1] It was understandable enough, then, why Marquand, after the success of *The Late George Apley*, should have turned to these New England scenes which he knew most intimately, for it was at the Mill that he came to live with his aunts at the age of fourteen when his parents were in the Canal Zone. In neighboring Newburyport he had attended high school, and from here he went on to Harvard.

For these reasons *Wickford Point* is the most obviously autobiographical of all his novels, and it is difficult to see his protagonist Jim Calder in any other guise than that of Marquand's alter ego—though, as in other Marquand novels, there is a bifurcation, with the author expressing himself by means of two writers, friends in the novel. Joe Stowe is the serious writer, recognized and acclaimed by the critics; Jim Calder is the popular one, the serialist, the craftsman who needed money and who couldn't take a chance on the big important novel. He is, we feel, Marquand before the success of *The Late George Apley.*

I *The Brills and Jim Calder*

"Wickford Point" is the ancestral home of the Brills, proud descendants of white-bearded old John Brill, the sage of "Wickford Point" and sometime friend and associate of New England transcendentalists—Emerson, Thoreau, Hawthorne, the Alcotts— and other New England worthies.[2] Jim Calder doesn't really belong, for though related to the family he is not a Brill. He is made to feel on numerous occasions that it is really too bad he cannot share the family name and mana, even though it was his grandfather who had prospered in New York and had made it possible for the feckless later generations of Brills to continue the traditions of "Wickford Point" through the trust fund he had set up to maintain the place.

But if Jim did not belong, he could still be used. The Brills, his Cousin Clothilde and his second cousins Bella, Sid, and Harry, welcome his arrivals at the "Point", for they know that he will be good for small loans to help them out of their endless financial difficulties, and that if there is no money for gasoline they may siphon it from Cousin Jim's car. They use his money, but they can hardly respect the means by which he obtains it; for, after all, as descendants of a now little-read and rather prosaic nature poet, they find it somehow dishonorable that Jim should be known to the world as a popular writer of serial stories for the mass-circulation magazines.

The present residents of "Wickford Point" live on the vanished glories of the past. They assume that, because they are Brills, the world must accept them at their own valuation. Their pride and self-complacency have been so carefully fostered that reality is seldom able to break through the web of illusion in which they have carefully wrapped themselves. This New England had once known a vigorous and dynamic society, but in the present something has gone out of it. Jim recalls to himself that there was a period, when his grandfather still lived, which was marked by security and a general sense of well-being at the "Point": "when the house had a clean soapy smell, when there were plenty of people in the kitchen to do the work, and two outside men to tend the garden and the grounds." When his grandfather was alive and before his Great-aunt Sarah's mind began to fail (in her last years she confused the generations in her mind, with the result that she often believed that the grandchildren were their parents or grandparents), life at "Wickford Point" had had direction and vitality. But, Jim observed, the "subsequent change was gradual, like the decline of the Roman Empire."

In Jim's day there were few domestics, and those who did remain were unpaid for weeks at a time, with the result that they all turned into "characters" and developed "personalities." Nothing ever got done. When a chair broke, it went unrepaired. The children lost the tools, and the gardens and drives went unweeded. If an aged and dying dog took possession of the landing on the front stairs, the family used the back stairs until the animal had died and been interred in the dog cemetery at the rear of the house. If a door stuck, the family used another door. When the clock struck nine, it was sure to be four hours slow.

Obviously the Brills couldn't go on like this—and yet they did. Cousin Clothilde spent her mornings in bed, calling the members of the family to her for long conversations of an aimless nature, smoking cigarettes provided by Jim, borrowing money when her bank account was overdrawn, as it was each month, for gin or ice cream or cigarettes. Years before, she had married Hugh Brill, son of old John Brill, the sage of "Wickford Point." They had had four children, Bella and Mary, Harry and Sid. Then, after Hugh Brill's death she had married Archie Wright; but Archie never really counted and he couldn't stand "Wickford Point" anyway. Therefore, during his lifetime, they had all lived in New York, taking one old house after another which they rented cheaply since they were shortly to be torn down to make way for new developments. Archie was always going to get a commission to paint a mural, but he never quite succeeded. And the children were always going to get jobs which never quite materialized.

Among the children was Harry, a Harvard man, who believed that the family name and the right connections could put him on easy street if only he played his cards right. He was the sort of snob who always attended parties, whether invited or not, since he couldn't conceive of his failure to receive an invitation as anything more than an inadvertent oversight on the part of the host. Younger brother Sid tinkered with useless inventions and suffered from chronic indigestion. Mary, the younger daughter, relentlessly pursued every man who appeared at

"Wickford Point" only to lose out as soon as the victim set eyes upon her sister Bella, the irresistible Bella, one of the bitchiest women to appear in modern fiction.

It has sometimes been said that Marquand couldn't portray women, that they are far less successful than his male characters, and generally speaking that is true. But in the creation of Bella "honey bee' Brill he suceeded in drawing an unforgettable portrait of a type of American woman which has become increasingly common in the galleries of novelists of a later generation. Jim Calder, who never quite frees himself of her influence even while understanding her motivations, perhaps more clearly than she does herself, characterizes her precisely when he declares:

> It was not difficult to think of her in a detached way, as though she were something which in no sense belonged in my life. I could think dispassionately of the beauty of her face and body, of her intuitive quickness, and of the indolence and intellectual superficiality which went with it. It was not hard to recognize that she was consumed by egotism and desires. The trouble was that her desires changed so fast that she could never be wholly sure of what she wanted—except that she wanted everything.

At first she had wanted—and married—Joe Stowe the writer and Jim's friend. But she could never get over the feeling that she was different from everybody else, she and the whole Brill family, and that no outsider was quite good enough for a Brill. To be sure, she protests frequently to Jim that she can't stand the family, that no one ever does anything but wish that something might be done. But that is no matter; it is a point of pride to the Brills, and to Bella in particular, that despite their eccentricities, their differences from other people, they are really set apart and distinguished by them. The marriage did not last, but Joe Stowe never quite got over it, and Jim Calder knows that his friend would come running to Bella if she should even crook a finger in his direction. "They tried to ruin me," Joe declared bitterly to Jim Calder. "They tried to take out my heart and lungs and liver and stuff me with sawdust."

When the novel begins, the reader suspects that Bella may choose any one of a half-dozen prospective mates. It might be her second cousin, Jim Calder; it might be a Wall Street broker named Howard Berg; she might decide to break up the marriage of Avery Gifford, a wealthy young Bostonian nothing, whom she had thrown over earlier for Joe Stowe; she might decide to remarry Joe Stowe; or—or she might even decide to go to Guatamala on an archeological expedition with a man named Dr. Frothinghope. But what she does, finally, is to take away from her sister Mary a Harvard professor named Allen Southby, appropriately enough described by Joseph Warren Beach as "a typical little academic pundit and pussy-cat, who has written a successful book of criticism and—poor dear—would like to write a novel."[3] And of all things, a novel about "Wickford Point"! Southby, when he receives guests in his Harvard apartment, serves them ale out of pewter tankards and permits the privileged few—Joe Stowe and Jim Calder—to read sections of his epic of the soil. Allen Southby is looking for tradition and seeking to forget his middle western past. His first sight of "Wickford Point" makes him realize that here is tradition that is just too precious, simply too superb; it is substance to give body to his idealizations of the New England cultural past.

Bella is ready for Allen Southby—or almost anything—because she has grown tired of being without money. At the time of her divorce she had refused alimony, presumably on principle, but when she abuses Joe Stowe to Jim Calder later she confesses that she had asked for nothing because he wasn't earning anything then. Now a successful writer earning $150,000 a year, he would do something for her if he were any kind of gentleman, particularly since, as she says, she doesn't even have the price of a dress. But Jim reminds her that Joe Stowe took a beating while he was with her and that now he is well out of the marriage and the whole Brill family. A moment later Bella can ask with incomparable innocence whether Jim thinks Joe still loves her, knowing very well that any man who has ever looked into her violet eyes and been smitten by her beauty has never quite recovered.

Perhaps Jim Calder managed to maintain a degree of objectivity toward Bella because of his conviction in his maturity that love makes marriage a highly dangerous business since neither party to the affair can be in anything approaching a normal state. All the good writers of the past, he concluded, had explored the condition of love and yet "had any gone any further than Tolstoy? Had they said as much as Jane Austen, who said exactly nothing?" He wondered whether it was not better to love from afar and in vain, or perhaps better to have one's love requited, and then when the disease (as he termed it) has passed, to marvel at the excessive nature of the expression and the feeling which has possessed one. Jim knows, and assures his friend Joe Stowe, that someone is always going to look out for Bella; but his feeling may be more than a little ambiguous when he asserts that if anyone takes care of Bella, it will be he, just as he's always taken care of the Brill family. He tells Joe Stowe that he is well out of it.

Marquand's own psychic wound, and his anomalous position in the contemporary world of letters, may show through his treatment of Jim Calder. Jim is conscious of the fact that he is called by his first name when the townspeople meet him, unlike the treatment received by the Brills. He was "almost a forgotten member of an ancient fellowship," but still a part of the town, just a local boy who had gone to the local high school, missing St. Swithin's which Harry had attended. At Harvard he, like Marquand, failed to make the better clubs and was excluded from the literary society—he and Joe Stowe, a fact which provided the original basis of their long friendship.

Reading Allen Southby's manuscript (Southby too had ignored him at Harvard), Jim is aware of the patronizing tone employed by the academic critic toward the popular writer who could hardly be expected to understand the subtler nuances of feeling and expression in the work of one like Dr. Southby, author of *The Transcendent Curve*. Marquand could, no doubt, from the vantage point of his first success, look back ironically, and a little bitterly, upon the experience of the pre-*Apley* writer. His revenge is taken in the wickedly malicious portrait of Allen Southby, a portrait which very nearly ends up as caricature. Conscious of no subtleties in Calder, Southby proves a largely unwitting victim of Calder's ironies. In the end he is reduced to the "academic pussy-cat" which Beach once termed him. In the end we know that he will get his Bella, and we discover him searching the library at "Wickford Point" for a volume of Chaucer so that he may read her "just a snatch from Sir Thopas, . . . a mirror to my mood:

> Alle othere wommen I foresake,
> And to an elf-queene I me take
> By dale and eek by downe!"

There are few satirical portraits in Marquand's work so unsparing. It was, we feel, a sweet revenge for Marquand, even though he came dangerously close to destroying his character's credibility in the process.

"Wickford Point" meant something special to Jim Calder, and what it meant we shall presently see. But when he left it to go into the Army and to France during World War I, he realized that, though he might see the place again and love it, still it would never be quite the same; the wound had been inflicted in the meantime at Harvard and before. He could never be the part of it which he had once been; "Wickford Point" could work no magic upon him where he was going, he thought, though he was finally proved mistaken. "It was," he said, "no shield to my sense of inferiority, because I did not possess the imagination to romanticize it. I felt that I was different, but unlike the Brills this knowledge gave me no sense of careless ease, and I was never able to use it as an adequate excuse for failure."

Looking back upon his past as an ante-bellum boy, the mature Jim Calder asserted that there had then existed a kind of snobbishness which was almost unbelievable, "although perhaps youth is still conventional when it has turned eighteen." Then he had felt the need to attach himself to something, to be a part of something, to be a particular kind of individual. Apologists say, Jim Calder agrees somewhat grudgingly, that the college is different now, that perfect spirit of democracy reigns; but personally he couldn't believe it. At Harvard he had been advised by his cousin Harry Brill that he shouldn't be seen about with a person like Joe Stowe, who didn't really belong and who could only hurt Jim's chances. When Jim failed to make Vindex, the literary club, there was little consolation in the fact that Joe Stowe hadn't made it either, though it brought them even closer together, and both pretended that it really didn't matter. Years later the mature Jim Calder could say, "The odd thing is that I can still feel a twinge of that old bitterness; for the hardest thing to live down is some ancient affront to vanity." In spirit the confession is not unlike that ambiguous tribute paid his old college by Marquand in his twenty-fifth anniversary report. To Jim there was some satisfaction, though hardly adequate, in the fact that both he and Joe Stowe, after they had achieved a measure of success, were addressed by their first names in the correspondence of the class secretary who had never spoken to them while they were in college.

Against such a background, it becomes easier to understand what "Wickford Point" meant to Jim Calder and also, to a lesser degree, to Joe Stowe. In childhood it had been a quiet haven of security, a little corner untouched by the world, a tie with a continuing tradition, a link with a meaningful past where in imagination one might touch the reality of receding generations. Aunt Sarah's wandering mind and her confusion of father with son was something Jim Calder could understand.

When he had first brought Joe Stowe home with him from Harvard, he was pleased, but not surprised, that Joe could enter into his Aunt Sarah's mood and accept the role which she had thrust upon him of a sea captain just returned from the Indies where he had touched at the exotic ports, with which the Brill mariners of a past era had been familiar. "Wickford Point" is a kind of destiny, a fate, as was family in *The Late George Apley*. There he had hunted woodcocks in the marshes and tidal flats, accompanied by the adolescent Bella. He had walked to the point and observed the rise and fall of the tides. Nothing really changed at "Wickford Point," despite the decadent and idle Brills who inhabited it, the Brills whom he loved—particularly Cousin Clothilde—no matter how feckless they might be. When he first took Joe there, he said, "I was feeling that old sort of anticipation which came over me every time I went down that hill, although nothing had ever come of it. I was feeling that old choking sense of loyalty for the place and a pleasure so intense in the idea that I was coming back that any obtuse remark of Joe's would have set my nerves on edge." It didn't very much matter that, if a door stuck, no one would attempt to repair it. The important thing was that life went on, somehow, at "Wickford Point" as if there were no intrusions from the outer world. Whenever he returned to "Wickford Point," he felt that "faraway, eerie quality coming back with the comfortable, musty smell of the warm side-entry," and with all the bedroom candles "safe on their shelf beside the chairs."

Wickford Point is a kind of New England idyl in spite of everything, in spite of the Brills, and even in spite of Dr. Allen Southby who presumably spent a great deal of time there following his marriage to Bella sometime after the novel ends. In the end, any road that Jim Calder took always seemed to turn toward home, and home was "Wickford Point." He couldn't forget it. Joe Stowe couldn't forget it either, even after the Brills had attempted to make a tame little pussy-cat of him. Reminiscently, Joe tells Jim in Boston: "There will be that same muddy smell from the river .... and the trees will be greener than anywhere else, and the humming birds will keep buzzing in the trumpet vines, and the plumbing will get out of order. And the tortoise-shell cat will have kittens and everybody will be unhappy in the parlor, and Sid will have indigestion and nobody will be able to stand it any longer."

Writing about the novel shortly after its appearance, Percy Holmes Boynton expressed the opinion that Marquand seemed to feel more affection for the Puritan Brills "gone to seed than he does for the ex-Puritan-Brahmin of the Apley type."[4] It may well be true, but if so, it is an affection strongly tinged with family loyalty; and above all it is a love of place. "Wickford Point" itself is the real object of his affection. In view of that feeling it is not difficult to understand Marquand's persistence in the long and bitter litigation with his relatives, the Hales, regarding their respective rights to the original of "Wickford Point." It was, after all, Jim Calder in the novel, much to the family's surprise, who inherited her share of the property from his Aunt Sarah.[5]

There is in *Wickford Point* a weaker impulse toward revolt on the part of the characters, for whom the place is both a curse and a destiny, than in any other Marquand novel; even Apley had to acknowledge inwardly from time to time the futility of his way of life. But in the unreal world which the Brills have created about them to evade the touch of reality, all is futility. Cousin Clothilde appears never to notice, or at least she never acknowledges, that she has increased the helplessness of her children in making them entirely dependent upon her by her absolute control of the monthly check from the estate's trustee. Her happiness, she tells Jim, comes from being able to meet to the best of her ability the requests of her children. Mary's despair grows from her failure to hold a man once he has seen sister Bella. Harry continually complains that he could handle the monthly income more capably than his mother if only he were permitted to make a budget for the family. Sid, the younger brother, seems quite content to borrow the clothes and to siphon the gasoline of his Cousin Jim.

Only Bella talks of revolt, and no one, certainly not Jim, really believes she means what she ways. Bella complains to Jim that she is going to hell, that she is getting just like all the other Brills, and to save herself she must get away. "God damn them all—except Clothilde!" she said. Jim's answer is that she has to be like them because she is one of them, and she

can't change that. Everyone at some time or other feels the
need to revolt against his environment, he tells himself, but in
Bella's case he dimly realizes that life is a trap for her because
she can't have everything. If she marries Avery Gifford, then
she can't have somebody else whom she might want more. She
wants everything, particularly if someone else also wants it—
someone like her sister Mary for example. But Jim hasn't quite
understood that Bella, as perhaps the most voluble of the Brills,
is really a coward. And it takes Patricia Leighton, who loves
Jim Calder and is waiting for him to marry her some day, to
make the Brills understandable to him. She feels at the end
that she has succeeded, at least in part, in removing some of
the scales from his eyes.

Patricia Leighton lives in a penthouse in New York and is
in charge of advertising for one of the large department stores.
Pat tells Jim Calder that he may move in anytime he wants to;
she wants to take care of him, she says. This character will be
recreated in *H. M. Pulham, Esquire* as Marvin Myles, who
wants to "take care" of Pulham too. But in the later book the
sum is refigured and Marvin loses; in the earlier novel, Patricia
wins. It is almost the only novel in which New England and
Cosmopolis or Vanity Fair achieve a resolution in understanding
and a happy ending.

So many people, Marquand's protagonists seem to illustrate,
never find it possible to finish what they have started. They
never realize the objectives which they set for themselves, or
they are forced to compromise for a partial victory. From novel
to novel the recurring refrain is that one can't have everything.
In *Wickford Point* the question raised is whether Jim Calder
can free himself from the almost painless bondage of family
and tradition and be his own man. The alternative is that he too
may become a Brill and no longer feel the need or the desire
to resist the lotus-land of the Brills.

The final answer is a compromise after all, for he will marry
Patricia Leighton but only with the understanding that he
may return to "Wickford Point" when he wishes. Pat Leighton
had told him that he couldn't get away from anything by thinking, and he knew that she was right about that. "There were
so many people who couldn't finish what they started. For
example, Harry Brill could never finish anything, nor Sid nor
Bella nor Mary. They were always starting something and then

dropping it. . . ." And Jim Calder knew that he must finish it, with Pat Leighton, if he were not to be a Brill.

Probably it was Pat's observation which finally freed him, from the family if not from the "Point." Jim had told her that he had no fear of her destroying him, because he knew she couldn't. They were both reasonably happy, and there was understanding between them. Take Bella for an example, Jim said, who was always afraid. And Pat's generalization was a startling observation. "Bitches are always afraid," she said. "You ought to be old enough to realize that every bitch is a coward." "Perhaps that's why they're bitches," Jim said. "I'd never thought of that." As for Aunt Clothilde, Pat suggested, she had put all the children in nice little houses, and she didn't intend to let them out for fear of losing them: "Perhaps a man can't understand it, but any woman would. If they changed, don't you see, she'd lose them? She couldn't do things for them any more—nice generous things. She wants to manage someone. She'd like to manage everyone because it means that she's doing something. That's why I want to manage you." And that was the way in which Jim Calder came to accept at least limited management, but he knew all the time that he loved "Wickford Point"— all the more so when he saw Allen Southby there. He could finally separate it from the family. He said, "I wanted to throw everyone out of it; I wanted it to be as it had been when Cousin Sue and Aunt Sarah were there" in the days before the "decline of the Roman Empire."

But Pat Leighton had recognized that nothing ever can be right if it always stays the same. It was her responsibility, a part of the "management" to force Jim Calder off dead center, to make him understand that one could not live in the past but only from the past. Permanence had to balance change—not deny the very existence of change. The Brills just went on and on, talking and complaining but resolving nothing. Jim had thought that he and Pat could go on in the same way, without decisions, without a change in their relationship, but her ultimatum, her either / or—"Wickford Point" or Pat Leighton—forces the decision. And so Pat Leighton wins, and presumably Jim Calder as well. His, however, is the final word when he says, "You heard what I said, that I'll always be there"; and she could accept the fact to salvage from the inertia of "Wickford Point" and the Brills the better part which she had claimed for her own.

II *Critical Reaction*

In writing of *Wickford Point* upon the book's appearance, most critics expressed admiration for the originality of structure, "like a braided Indian basket," Percy H. Boynton wrote, "spiraling from bottom to rim, firmly interwoven, but dizzying to follow. . . ."[6] And dizzying it is indeed. Despite the novelty at that time in Marquand's use of the flash-back, the reader of the later novels will be aware of the not entirely successful experimentation with a technique which he was to perfect and make uniquely his own. Though he was to use the device of counterpointing present and past time in all of his novels—perhaps most successfully in *Point of No Return* and *Melville Goodwin, U.S.A.*—Marquand often seems more than a little uncertain of time relationships in *Wickford Point,* and the reader is occasionally rather surprised by the sequences employed. And yet such critics as Boynton and Joseph Warren Beach were understandably impressed by Marquand's handling of his material. It is a comparative judgment, after all. Had we not been in a position to weigh Marquand's accomplishment in this novel against his achievement in those which were to follow, we might very well have concurred in the uniform admiration of the earlier critics.

It is more difficult to understand the objections of those critics who pointed to Marquand's deftness and skill while apparently feeling that he would have been a better novelist had he not written so well. Joseph Warren Beach objected to what he called Marquand's "stagy cleverness" in dialogue, and he wondered "whether it is possible for genius to be so good in the drawing room."[7] But surely the objection has little point. We have, no doubt, been for too long a time influenced in our critical judgments by the naturalistic tradition; and it is probable that the novel of manners, even as modified by writers of the twentieth century, has become so unfamiliar in our time that we hardly know how to regard a writer like John P. Marquand. But we almost certainly would not wonder about Jane Austen whether it is possible "for genius to be so good in the drawing room."

Wickford Point will probably not be regarded in the final judgment as the best of Marquand's novels, though such was the judgment of Maxwell Geismar.[8] But for the admirer of his work it will remain one of the most interesting and, for those who knew the author, the most memorable in every sense. As Marquand's friend Edward Weeks, editor of the *Atlantic Monthly,* wrote in tribute: "There is loneliness and hurt and love (the love for Kent's Island, which eventually became his own home place) in *Wickford Point,* and somehow, in the fast crisp prose of the book, I have the feeling that the author is speaking to me more intimately than in any other."[9]

CHAPTER 4

"I guess I've always been a 'straight'"

CENTRAL to the Marquand ethos is the novel many readers have considered his greatest, *H. M. Pulham, Esquire*. The dust jacket quite misses the point, as dust jackets so often do, when it asserts that the book is Marquand "at his brilliant, satiric best—the biting story of a rich, proper Bostonian who fell in love with a girl who didn't belong." But the point of a Marquand novel is that it is never quite clear who *does* belong and who does not.

It seems unfortunate that *Pulham*, like other Marquand novels, should so often be read in narrowly social terms, for it is the human situation of which we should be aware; it is the universal application of transmuted experience which should strike us. Though, as we have seen, the autobiographical element in his novels is hardly negligible, it is certainly true, as he tells us in his note prefacing *Pulham*, that "living men and women are too limited, too far from being typical, too greatly lacking in any universal appeal, to serve in a properly planned piece of fiction." His characters, he unnecessarily assures us, present the thoughts of a certain social group, "not limited to Boston or Cambridge, since this group exists in every other large community." If we associate those qualities of a stubborn integrity displayed by Harry Pulham in the course of the novel with a New England tradition, they are at the same time really no different essentially from the fidelity, the courage and endurance, and the loyalty which find expression in the work of the Conrads and the Jameses and the Whartons, irrespective of any considerations of class or status.

I *The Examined Life*

Pulham, then, is very much more than the "biting story of a rich, proper Bostonian who fell in love with a girl who didn't belong." And if "biting," it is often rather difficult to determine who gets bitten. Marquand is only incidentally, and certainly not primarily, a satirist. We suspect that in this novel, as in all his better work, Time is the biter and all the characters, like the reader himself, are the victims. No one of Marquand's generation wrote more poignantly of inexorable time, of mutability, of the flood of the largely wasted years. Every major Marquand character becomes sadly aware of a "point of no return."

It is the examined life and only the examined life which has significance in the novels of Marquand, even though the examinations seem to grow less meaningful at the end of his career. Charles Brady sees truly that the settings of Marquand's novels are Newburyport, Boston, Cambridge, New England and New York—anywhere, anytime, really—and that the characters are always, and alternately, a younger Marquand who repeatedly ponders "The roads that diverge in a yellow wood, while an older Marquand, all too poignantly conscious of the road he took, yet cannot forget the road not taken."[1]

The point that distinguishes Marquand as a satirist is that he was first a very great lover. His satirical portraits are never etched in acid, and we feel that Marquand the man never quite dissociates himself from the object of his examination. When we become aware, for example, that Harry Pulham's curious obtuseness in the matter of his personal relationships leaves him vulnerably naked in our eyes, we almost inevitably find ourselves at his side, as no doubt Marquand did also. We find ourselves loving the "straight" because the world is so largely populated by the wise and knowing ones, those deprived of all their innocence. It is Bill King, Harry Pulham's friend, the rootless and despairing modern, who says that Harry has always been a "straight" and must, no doubt, always be one. A "straight," Bill explains, is he who feeds the lines to the witty one; and Harry concedes that he has probably always been a "straight." "Maybe," Bill replies, "but maybe it's better than being the smart man. He's mighty lonely and there're lots and lots of straights."

There are lots of "straights," and Harry Pulham was one of the most decent ones. As the eve of the twenty-fifth anniversary of his graduation from Harvard draws near, he is brought together with other graduates by Bo-Jo Brown, the activist, the one most likely to succeed, the all-round athlete. As Harry admits on that occasion to another of the graduates gathered together to plan the reunion, he wonders what Brown could want of him: "I have never had ideas."

And indeed he had not. For Harry was a very ordinary sort of fellow. It is his story that Marquand tells, introducing from time to time the events of the period and the contemporary head-lines—from World War I, Harding, the "return to normalcy," to Czechoslovakia, appeasement, all the rest of it—which place Harry in time, and a troubled one at that. As an old-fashioned "straight," Harry, without knowing it, belongs to the humanist tradition. In a world of rapid change and declining values, he clings to the belief in decency and in fidelity; he does so not from any abiding philosophical conviction that in that way man may resist the swirling nihilistic currents of his time, the relativity of all values, but simply because there seems no other decent and practical course to be pursued.

Marquand himself comes at what appears to be the end of a traditional faith in humanistic values; his ambivalent attitude is reflected in his dichotomizing of his characters. Marquand is Harry Pulham, the believer in tradition; but he is also the root-less Bill King. This division enables the artist to write with gentle mockery of the thing he innately loves, and the resulting effect is a curious tentativeness of judgment. As Phillip Ham-burger has truthfully asserted about Marquand: ". . . one had to love something solid, real, and permanent before one could bring oneself to satirize it."[2] Conclusions in the Marquand novels are highly tentative because Marquand never quite escapes the same bafflement felt by Pulham regarding the examined life. Harry, contemplating the prospect of writing his own brief biography for the Class Book at the twenty-fifth reunion, thinks of the before-and-after class picture, of young men in high collars as they appeared in the first class report placed beside the pictures of the men twenty-five years later: "bald-headed, gray-bearded, weary—and what had it all been about?"

What had it all been about? Harry Pulham in the course of the novel seeks to find out. As he reads the barren recital of business and family relationships in a report submitted by yet another graduate of another class, he asks if such a report is characteristic and he is assured that it is.

Time is a trap from which no Marquand character ever makes his escape, though the unimaginative, the former football heroes like Bo-Jo Brown, may accomodate themselves so completely to the encumbrances that they are hardly aware of their predica-ment. But if life traps its victims, and we must finally do what it was meant all along that we should do, it is still possible to consider the knowledge of what might have been, the road not traveled by. In *H. M. Pulham, Esquire,* Harry and his friend Bill King complement each other. Harry represents the clinging to whatever values of order and balance remain in a crumbling tradition; Bill, the fluidity and change, the volatility of a culture which has largely abandoned the sense of absolutes. Without ties to tradition or a sense of purpose beyond the pursuit of the bitch goddess success, Bill can never accept the presentness of the past nor the unaltering standards even though, cleverer than his friend Harry, he recognizes his rootlessness with a poignant anguish.

Marquand has supplied each with a familiar theme, a recurring tag-line, which is his respective leitmotif. Bill King asserts repeatedly: "I suppose it's what I'm meant for—here today and gone tomorrow." Harry is characterized by the flat finality of of his "Why, yes, of course!" The "of course" expresses the certainty of the sun's rising and setting, the enduring and unquestioned verities. Harry Pulham is almost the Last Puritan and the last Emersonian idealist, a bit of both in a continuing tradition.

Harry heads his own investment firm in Boston where his life has settled into a comfortable pattern of an unquestioning (or only occasionally questioning) conformity. But he has known his unquiet hours. Following a respectable New England childhood there had been the private schooling at St. Swithin's, then Harvard, and a brief but not undistinguished career of a lieutenant in France during World War I. Finally, there was his return, the unsettledness and the quiet revolt against family and tradition which had taken him to New York and the beginning of a career in advertising under the aegis of his Harvard friend, Bill King. And, most significantly, there had been the love which had developed between him and the girl in the office, Marvin Myles.

"For once in my life," Harry says, "I was where I wanted to be, a part of everything." And he hadn't ever quite managed to achieve the feeling before, despite St. Swithin's with its headmaster known as "The Skipper," despite the standards of his home with his mother and his sister Mary, and above all his father who, Harry confesses on one occasion, was rather "like required reading, something you faced with a sense of duty and were rather surprised if it interested you." It was not a background against which it was easy to rebel, though Harry could envy the easy rebellion of Bill King at Harvard and after, of Bill who didn't really belong at all and who expressed the coldest contempt for all the flawless father-images in Harry's New England background.

Bill never could understand. To him the Skipper was "that old jelly fish . . . a conceited, pandering poop." And the students, the products of St. Swithin's, were caught young and shaped into a pattern which he developed. He could never understand Harry's contention that there were a lot of things that one never could say goodby to if one went to a first-rate school.

Despite the family, the training, the years at Harvard, Harry never really felt that he belonged. He had come closest to the feeling at prep school when he felt he was "an integral part of something—a part of the group." But he never really "made the team." And as Harry confessed about Harvard many years later: "I always say that Harvard is the most democratic institution in the world, but secretly I do not believe it. . . ." Even so, at Harvard he met Bill King, and while this new acquaintance was never quite acknowledged by the other boys of the group, Harry found it quite impossible to repulse the friendly overtures made to him by this "outsider" who came from some place in New Jersey. "You're the first person I've seen here who isn't a nickel-plated son of a bitch," Bill declared bitterly. And Harry was honest enough to confess that he had "an uneasy feeling that I was doing something out of the ordinary, that I was associating with someone dubious, but still I was pleased."

It was probably Bill King who was responsible for keeping alive a small flame of rebellion in Harry's breast. When Harry took him home from Harvard for Sunday lunch, the parents acted in the unaccountable way they always acted; his mother invited an acceptable girl, one of their kind, "a dear, sensible girl," his mother said. "She's one of those girls who doesn't think about herself, or think about her looks. She thinks of other people." To Harry at the time she was a "lemon," even if he was fated to marry her years later. To Bill, Harry apologized for the "awful" Sunday lunch, but Bill reassured him by saying it was like similar occasions everywhere else. "It's sad," Bill said, "because they try so hard." Bill was clever, he knew, and he himself was not. It had always been somewhat that way. But Harry had never quite lost the sense of life as a game in which, as the Skipper had said, one had to show "fight, always show fight."

When Harry returned to New York, found the job at the

advertising agency, and fell in love with Marvin Myles, he felt as though he had finally "made his letter"; he was a part of the team. He was part of everything, even though his employer couldn't decide whether he was "dumb or clever." But the nicest thing that had ever been said to him, Harry concluded, was Marvin's assertion that he wasn't either one or the other: "You're just yourself. I've never seen anyone like you." But Marvin realizes, as Harry cannot, that he doesn't really belong on the team which is engaged in a feverish campaign to sell soap. Seeing pictures of his father, his mother, and his sister Mary on his dresser as she helps him pack for a visit at home, Marvin observes "All of you is there, isn't it? All that you're going back to? It must be queer, being in two places at once."

Harry doesn't know what she is talking about. Back home there is almost equal difficulty in reaching any understanding with his father, who cannot accept that, in the midst of change and the restlessness of change, there could ever be a question of some things changing or being lost—"such as common decency and civilization and human liberty." The father, who is not very good at words, as Harry says, expresses views which the son was never able to understand until years later when, he confesses, a lot of his own beliefs and standards "too vague to specify" were washed overboard. He tells his son: "It isn't any news that any of us are going to die, but we like to think we're going to be remembered. We don't like to see everything we believe in changing. I should hate, for instance, to feel that the world is going to stay as topsy-turvy as it is. I know it isn't going to. You and everybody else are going to settle down, because certain values can't change." At least they cannot, in the father's opinion, if one determines that they shall not. The elder Pulham wonders that Harry should welcome the opportunity to assert the integrity of a soap product, an integrity built upon half-truths and outright falsehoods, that he should welcome it just because in that shadowy world something was always happening. Harry's father says: "I can't recall ever wanting things to happen. I've spent all my life trying to fix it so that things wouldn't happen."

Harry returned to New York, even though he wasn't being "regular," even though the decision struck his father like a blow. Though Marvin was not of his own kind, he knew that he would have to return to her. A new liberated female making a career for herself in the competitive man's world of business, Marvin could tell Harry that, while she loved him, the office was a place for business; intimate moments were reserved for the hours of relaxation at home. In New York Harry realized that he was moving swiftly away from everything that he had ever known, that he was embarked upon an adventure for which he had no directives. He confessed that "Marvin was a good deal more of a person than I was, more talented, more cultivated, but I realized very suddenly that I was facing something like the Army—a different sort of life—and that my training was entirely inadequate."

Nothing of the kind had ever happened to Harry before; he was convinced that it could never happen again. Everything between him and Marvin was unique. When they became lovers, Harry had been little aware of the initiative taken by Marvin in bringing about their intimacy. He was prepared to apologize for so far forgetting himself, knowing that she probably couldn't help hating him. Certainly that would have been the response for which his mother's training had prepared him. And he was as certainly not prepared for Marvin's response: "'Why you damn fool!' Marvin said, 'you sweet, dear damn fool!'" Then, Harry said, "Everything was all right. It was what I've always felt—that everything was always all right whenever Marvin was there."

II   Clash of Traditions

Marvin's feeling is rather more complex. In her realization of the worlds which separate her from all that Harry Pulham represents, the reader becomes aware of the clash of the traditional and the traditionless, of the relative and shifting values of one segment of the divided culture and the changeless and absolute values of the other. Bill belongs to the same world as Marvin, a fact dimly understood by Harry, who sometimes wonders why Marvin should prefer him to Bill. What he does not understand is that he is secure in the possession of some quality of certitude which both Bill and Marvin covet. And most of Pulham's critics miss the point when they fail to understand the quality of Harry Pulham and wonder why Marvin should find something to love in him. Marvin is jealous because Harry drives a car so effortlessly; because he plays tennis so well, having been taught from the age of eleven; because everything seems so effortless for him, so much taken for granted. "I know the whole secret of Marvin Myles"—Harry declares in a moment of rare percipience—"that she wanted things to belong to her, because what belonged to her gave her a sense of well-being. . . . Once something belonged to her, she would give it everything she had. I know, because I once belonged to her." Or as Marvin herself says on another occasion, "It makes me frightened when I see you doing things that I can't do. They take you away from me, all those little things."

And Bill, in the same way, clings to Harry because he seems to offer some kind of moorings, a sense of stability missing from his own topsy-turvy world. Harry imagines that Bill talks so much about College, about all of Harry's friends—Bo-Jo Brown and Sam Green and Joe Bingham and the rest—who had never been Bill's friends, because he likes to argue. For Harry insists over and over that Bill had never really known them; they weren't *really* stuffed shirts, Harry declares, but without ever recognizing that, whatever the limitations of these friends, Bill is expressing not contempt for their qualities but envy of their assurance, of their sense of belonging. "If it hadn't been for me," Bill asserts possessively again and again, "you wouldn't be down here, boy. I'm the best friend you ever had." Bill King, idea man behind the campaigns for selling soap and men's suspenders—Bill King, who knew all kinds of people, actors and headwaiters and playwrights and taxidrivers—was the real friend, not those stuffed shirts with whom Harry had grown up and who shared, almost as if by instinct, a common and unalterable set of values.

On the other side, Harry's world seemed to lack much of the smartness, the sophisticated polish which characterized Cosmopolis and Vanity Fair. When Harry took Marvin to a Harvard game and they met some of Harry's friends, he could see that she was the best-dressed woman there; and Marvin remarked that Kay Motsford, whom Harry had known since childhood and who was now engaged to Joe Bingham, would be a very pretty girl if only she knew how to dress. Again, when Harry's father and his sister Mary came up to the city for a visit, Harry found himself wishing that Marvin "could take Mary out and do something about her clothes." He knew that Mary was "trying to be smart and wasn't doing it very well. Her dress had a ready-made look and her coat was not properly tailored—suddenly I felt sorry for her. I wanted her to have a good time."

There was the world of the city, the world of shifting values, in which there seemed always to be the possibility of new starts, of fresh beginnings; then there was the world in which one recognized only one chance, the one road taken, and to speak of a second chance was, as Father Pulham said, "just damned rot." But there was the possibility that in such a world, as Mary Pulham ruefully suggested, "some people never have a chance at all."

This point is central to the novel, to this and to other Marquand novels as well. For Marquand sounds the "Dear Brutus" theme again and again: The fault lies in ourselves, not in our stars, that we are underlings. But often the fault appears, after all, to lie in our stars; and in *Pulham* the characters consider that second chance before they finally reject the possibility and resign themselves to the road once taken.

Marquand is concerned, here as elsewhere, with the theme of time, which traps and cheats as often as it fulfills. Recalling those months in New York, Harry thinks of the meaning of time. When he first knows of his love for Marvin, she tells him that for once in his life he is going to be happy. And she asks: "Have you ever really been?" He repeats the word, as though it meant nothing in itself, as though he had never heard of such a question being asked, as if the quality of being were an abstract absolute good. He replies rather doubtfully that he supposes he never really has been happy. But then, there seemed to be enough time, for he had never felt the compulsive need to seize time by the forelock, or to make it run if he could not make it stand still. On this occasion he wonders "what would have happened if I had not kept thinking that there were lots of time. Time has always seemed to me to move strangely, now swiftly and now slowly, and all that time with Marvin Myles gives me the impression of looking from the window of a train which is hastening through some country that I have always wanted to see."

But he never did get to see that country. When a call came from home reporting the grave illness of his father, he and Bill King went at once by train. When Bill said that he couldn't understand why Kay Motsford would want to marry a "big drink of cold water" like Joe Bingham, Harry said that she was very plain, and Bill wondered how he could possibly say such a thing about Kay Motsford. But that was almost the last show of resistance to the life that he had attempted to leave behind; soon he was to marry Kay Motsford without ever knowing what Bill felt for her, without realizing that to Bill she represented the same permanence and stability in a world of change that Marvin Myles had found in Harry Pulham.

In the last interview with his father, Harry hears the dying man urge him to "live," repeating the note of James's Strether in *The Ambassadors.* " 'Don't,' he said, 'put it off. Do what you want to do. . . . You know what I mean?' he asked. 'What you want to do.' " But the invitation came too late, if there ever had been time for it. After the elder Pulham's death Harry received the letter from Marvin which he was to keep through the years buried between the pages of volume three of *Plutarch's Lives,* without ever understanding until the years had passed what she really meant. We could never quarrel, she said, but "when you're up there all alone . . . it isn't so bad if you know you have someone, someone, forever and always, someone you can always come back to. . . ."

But at home there were all the details of the estate; there was also the need to be concerned about Mary's affair with a dentist named Priest whom no amount of wishing could possibly turn from a dentist into a doctor. Even Harry's sister saw that he was more and more like his father: "Sometimes," she said, "you can be the damnedest fool. I wish you'd shut up." These were all reasons for his staying on, but finally he had to admit to himself: "There were dozens of similar complications that seemed to wind around me, but I can't think of them all as excuses now and none of them as real reasons why I stayed. I stayed because I was meant to stay."

There were some things gentlemen did not do: they did not kiss and tell, for example. And they were contemptuous of cry-babies. So one did one of two things: one took what was coming to him—"like a Gentleman, as the Skipper used to say at School"— or one revolted. And the latter course could and often did lead to all manner of impossible situations. One might become what Harry's friends called a "mess." He became, for instance, a Socialist, the way Bob Carroll finally did, or else he just went around hating everybody and seeing queer people. Certainly nothing more irresponsible than that could be imagined under any circumstances. "When I was hurt so badly that sometimes life did not seem worth living," Harry says, "I did not want anyone to know it, or even to take it up with myself."

Playing squash with Joe Bingham almost every afternoon, slipping back to his desk at the bond house of Smith and

Wilding, and trying as hard as possible to live the life which everyone around him lived—all this activity helped Harry to escape the shadow of Marvin Myles. ("'I don't want to sell bonds,' I said. 'My boy,' said Mr. Wilding, 'no one wants to, but that's the way we live.'") It all seemed joyless enough at best, but Harry had concluded that "there is nothing worse than being too much involved in yourself." He saw a good deal of Kay Motsford, who seemed happy enough despite her broken engagement, though she did inquire frequently about Bill King and never could understand why he was so busy that he didn't seem to be able to come for a visit. Of course, the engagement of Joe Bingham and Madeline Bush had come as something of a surprise, even to Joe, but Kay Motsford said that was the way it was; a woman knew about it before the man did. And there were other marriages in the old group, with Harry acting as usher and Kay as a bridesmaid.

Bill finally came down once more, and Harry asked about Marvin; but Bill only said she was all right and that Harry needn't worry about her. He seemed less interested in Harry's life. "'Bill,' I said, 'you're not mad at me, are you?' I felt about him, I suppose, much the way Joe Bingham felt about me." Bill said that he had been but wasn't anymore, and then he wondered if maybe Kay wasn't mad at him because she seemed so cool. It was like women, he said, to build up a trivial incident in their imaginations. But Harry didn't know what he was talking about or why Bill should have said that women don't seem to realize "that you're here today and gone tomorrow."

Thrown more and more together, Harry and Kay were almost destined, by propinquity if for no other reason, to wed. "There is nothing easier than doing something Nature wants you to do," so Harry concluded, "and there is always someone ready to help you." He found it hard to agree with the romantic novelists who always suggested that there was considerable difficulty in finding someone to marry. In the case of Harry and Kay they both decided that it was difficult to attempt being something different from what they were. It just didn't work. But as Harry confessed to himself, when he looked at the matter honestly, he had to admit that "Kay was only a symbol in a problem and that I was the same to her." Harry, with his practical view of romance and marriage, was not greatly troubled since he had come to feel that "It is what happens after marriage, the method two people find of getting on with each other, that is really important."

III   *A Novel about Marriage*

Pulham is, first and foremost, a novel of marriage and of love in marriage; there has probably been no novelist of our time who has written more understandingly, more perceptively, of the marital relationship than has Marquand in this novel. As one of Marquand's critics has pointed out, each of the major characters, each of his heroes, "has a Beatrice somewhere in his past; and . . . each of them, in his own Puritan way, manages to escape the romantic hell of Paolo and Francesca. Like the Roman in Dante, the Roman in Marquand knows that, in some circumstances, romance is a pander and so are writers of romance."[3] The Roman in Harry Pulham would have agreed had the subtlety of the comparison not escaped him. Harry believed then, and he believed more firmly some twenty years after his marriage, that love was probably after all simply a matter of "not passion or wish, but days and years."

When he knew that he would marry Kay, it was as though it had always been and was always meant to be. The card he received from Marvin Myles asking, "Darling, aren't you coming back?"— that card he could ignore when he had about him all the reminders of a way of life which could never change. He knew that he was never going back because he also knew that in the most important sense he had never been away. There was no one now but the two of them, Harry and Kay, and he felt as though he had been struggling through a wood and had finally come out into the sun.

Such were the events of Harry's past which he recalled on the eve of the twenty-fifth anniversary of his graduation from Harvard. Bill had been the best man at his wedding, Bill who said that among his New York friends "not one of them is married—not seriously." It was the same with him, whose marriage to Elise did not last; and like them, his friends in New York, it was what he was meant for, "here today and gone tomorrow." On the honeymoon, Kay, who had always thought she wanted the things Boston could not give her, who had always longed for the kind of romance which the books described and which Bill King, in imagination, provided—Kay said, "Darling, it's just a little thing, but could you just stop saying 'of course' "? She might have been prepared for Harry's answer: "Why, yes, Kay. Of course."

For the reunion of the class Bill came down from New York.

Before he arrived, Harry became ill from food poisoning. Kay had to entertain Bill, and Harry was more of a "straight" than ever. But as Harry explained to Bill:

> All the things that two people do together, two people like Kay and me, add up to something. There are the kids and the house and the dog and all the people we've known and all the times we've been out to dinner. Of course Kay and I do quarrel sometimes, but when you add it all together, all of it isn't as bad as the parts of it seem. I mean, maybe that's all there is to anybody's life.

But it wasn't all that Kay hoped for, and the joyless adultery with Bill King during his visit never permitted her to forget the "hours and days." It was quite impossible to overcome the simplistic view of life which Harry entertained, the simple loyalties and the unswerving faith, and the conviction that even in his reading there was a standard which had to be met. Harry could not understand or sympathize with the characters of the modern novel who were "always struggling with internal emotional conflicts that revealed themselves in sexual irregularities, and they were never anyone I knew." There were never "decent honest-to-goodness men or women," like Harry Pulham or his friend Bill King or his own wife.

From time to time Harry has a feeling, which he had when he was younger, that he had never really seen the world—not clearly at any rate. But the point is made that innocence is perhaps the best protection against a world in which only sorrow and disillusionment and frustration await the individual who is too knowingly aware. Ignorance is a kind of bliss so far as Harry Pulham is concerned, and perhaps, ironically, in the world which Harry Pulham inhabits only ignorance can make that world tolerable. Harry is never aware of the evasions with which Bill or Kay confront him. And it is in the midst of this guilty betrayal on the part of his wife and his best friend that he again discovers Marvin Myles, and that Kay discovers the letter from Marvin, written so many years before. She is surprised that her husband might ever have had another love—good, safe Harry, who was "always being careful, always being safe, only wanting to see the same people because it isn't any effort, always being dull."

The difference between Harry and Bill is summarized by a conversation they have during the reunion. Bill says: "Life is made up of working and living and loving, of women and money, and God knows what! But it hasn't got anything to do with what you learned when you were a boy." And Harry's reply characterizes him: "'I don't know,' I said, 'I suppose you'll think this is funny, but a good deal of life is playing the game.'" Bill and Harry hardly speak the same language, but Bill, guiltily, understands—what Harry does not— when his friend says: ". . . there are rules in it. You can take the Decalogue, for instance—about coveting your neighbors' wife and his ox and his ass." And Bill says that he never coveted oxen or asses, but—with his face red—"a good many rather decent people commit adultery. You know the rules and you break them. Boy, you'd be surprised."

But the rules are there in the breach as well as in the observance. If Harry doesn't understand, he is willing to attribute his values to his friend. "I simply mean that you and I, Bill, we have our rules." Finally Harry knew that he could not accept Bill's rules or Bill's principles in a life made up of making money and making women. There was a good deal more to it than that. "Life," he decided, "is made up of letting the dog out, of hitting your thumb with the hammer when you were driving nails, of getting someone to fix the washer in the laundry faucet, of Christmas and friends to dinner—of thousands of things like that all added up together."

When Harry meets Marvin again at the reunion, after Marvin has married a wealthy member of the class who, Bill once asserts, is something of a "straight" like Harry, she asks him again whether he is happy. Harry wonders how anyone can answer such a question, but he decides that he must say, "Yes, yes, I've been happy, Marvin." And no doubt he had, though as he thinks of the question he concludes that one might have gone a great deal further, inquiring what happiness is. "The question in itself and the answer," he decides, "had no particular validity. I was struggling with what had come between us, and I knew what it was. It was time. There had been so much time, a whole road of it." And it was the road not taken. When he asks Marvin if she has had what she wanted she replies "nearly everything." But then Harry concludes that one can never have everything. It is an echo of the question that Harry asks Bill: Have you had everything you want? Bill's answer is that no one ever has everything. No one can have everything. Finally, Harry's answer is the best answer, or so Marquand leads us to believe.

As a novelist of marriage, or of love in marriage, Marquand in *Pulham* (and in his other serious works) is as far from the clichés of popular magazine fiction as it is possible for a serious writer to be. As Mr. Brady has pointed out, "in the end Kay learns that kindness is not a bad substitute for the ecstasy which is rarely for sale in the booths of Vanity Fair."[4] And so far as Harry is concerned, by his example he demonstrates as conclusively as one could wish that "when all is said and done, innocence remains the greatest shield of man in his vale of sorrow, the world."[5] He realizes that he had lived, all things considered, "the only sort of life for which I was really fitted." The result of his meeting with Marvin Myles was that he achieved a recognition of the illusory character of "passion and wish," that he realized he could not have gone back to the road not traveled by, even if he had finally wished to, "because Kay and I had been so long together."

As he concluded about himself, he was "not bright or quick or clever," but he could take what was coming to him. It had really all been finished nearly twenty years before. And he was clever enough, brighter perhaps than the Bill Kings and the really clever ones of the world, and well able to realize that the search for variety, the need to be "here today and gone tomorrow," and the continual frustrations of the Madame Bovarys of the world were all the result of believing that one could go back, that perhaps after all love was not days and years but "passion and wish."

One could not go back; one could only go home, to the knowledge that the pilot light in the gas range was out again, that the front door key had "a big notch at the base and then two little notches" so that one could find it in the dark, that the dog would want putting out. And entering his house silently he could hear through the closed parlor door the voices of Bill and Kay, the voice of Kay saying, as though echoing his thoughts, "Let's not go all over it again. We can't go back." For the briefest moment there flashed across his mind the thought that perhaps there was something between Kay and Bill, "such as people talk about sometimes." He dismissed the thought at once, but then he knew he had no business having such an idea, for "Bill King was my best friend, and besides he was a gentleman, and Kay was my wife. As I say, I was ashamed of myself. It made me feel like apologizing to both of them when I opened the parlor door, and I told myself I must never consider such a thing again—not ever."

Like an echo, too, is Bill's response to Harry's inquiry whether he has everything he wants. " 'That's a damned silly question,' Bill said, 'and you know it, boy. Nobody ever has everything he wants.' " Bill must return to New York at once, Kay says, looking so distressed that Harry concludes she has really been working too hard attempting to entertain Bill. Besides, her hands are cold, and Harry thinks she may need a hot water bag. " 'Anything,' she said, 'anything but a hot water bag.' " And in another restatement of the theme, of which they are both aware, Kay remarks how funny it is—how funny that one must keep going on, "how you can't go back." When he helps her up, she kisses him, and Harry thinks it very generous of her.

Kay has had her joyless adultery, and it is all rather dreadful, as she understands that there is no going back. She says, "the only thing that matters is you and me." And so it is. It is resolution and reconciliation, though Harry never quite understands that it is the latter.

Even Kay was finally ready to accept the inevitability of the phrase. "Of course" was probably more enduring and permanent than "here today and gone tomorrow." And to Harry it was a strange coincidence that both Kay and Marvin had used that other phrase, the one about not being able to go back. "Even their voices had sounded alike," he recalls. "I did not know to what Kay was referring and probably she hardly knew herself, because she was so tired that she had just said whatever had come into her mind. Kay always did use up her strength when it came to entertaining. She had seen too much of Bill. He had so much vitality that he exhausted even me sometimes. But still it was a coincidence."

It seems quite the proper time to finish that autobiographical sketch for the twenty-fifth year book since the house is quiet and his thoughts had been dwelling so continuously in the past during recent days. He decides that he had better leave out the bit about being decorated in the war "because there is nothing worse than showing off." And he concludes with the expectation that neither Mr. Roosevelt or Germany "can hold out much longer," and he looks forward to seeing soon a sensible Republican in the White House.

IV *Skill of Marquand*

The reconciliation scene between Harry and Kay Pulham is certainly one of the finest and truest in contemporary literature. Probably Marquand did none better and few as well. It is difficult to understand why Marquand has failed to receive the critical recognition he deserves for such perceptive writing, or why the recognition he has received should have been so grudgingly given. Marquand's handling of this final resolution suggests comparisons. There is fatality in Harry Pulham's conclusion that "there is some needle inside everyone which points the way he is to go without his knowing it." The ending of Mrs. Wharton's *Age of Innocence* comes to our mind, for Newland Archer recognizes the "needle" within himself which has pointed the way he was to go all along; and, knowing that there has been too much time between him and Madame Olenska, he cannot go back. Newland Archer, after watching the shades being drawn across the windows of the woman he had once loved so greatly, rises slowly and walks back alone to his hotel. Both men, Newland Archer and Harry Pulham, preferred in the end to keep their memories locked up in a small room of the mind as something apart, more real on the outside, as Archer said, than if he had gone up to that shuttered drawing-room, than if he had made the impossible attempt to go back to the road not traveled by.

We are particularly struck by the extraordinary skill and sureness of touch displayed by Marquand in his treatment of this scene when we compare it with the handling of another "reconciliation" by a novelist like Sinclair Lewis, who is also sometimes spoken of as a novelist of manners. There are, of course, some rather obvious points of comparison between *Babbitt* and *H. M. Pulham, Esq.* Both novels are concerned in some degree with the issue of rebellion versus conformity, though it is George Babbitt in the first and Kay Pulham in the second who are the principal rebels against a way of life which they have begun to find stifling. Harry Pulham, to be sure, had revolted briefly against his family and his background before his marriage. But it was never necessary for him to prove himself an individualist, a free-thinking "liberal," as it had been for George Babbitt. The Pulhams, their friends and associates, are never marked by the vulgarities of the various representatives of the social strata in Zenith; and there is a vastly greater complexity and subtlety

of situation and motivation in the Marquand novel. *Babbitt,*
by comparison with *Pulham,* will seldom seem to rise above the
level of caricature, of one-dimensional characterization. But
Harry Pulham and George Babbitt share, in different degrees,
the conviction that they do not really "belong." Pulham feels
that he never really was a part of things, though he is reconciled
to his place through an acceptance of the obligations of duty and
loyalty; Babbitt, who feels himself shut out from the full acceptance by the members of the upper-upper-middle class, rebels
briefly but finally is forced, by public pressure and threatened
ostracism, to play the game of the leading Zenith businessmen.

Both Babbitt and Pulham, too, "breed children whom they
do not understand. And who will never understand them." Or
so we are led to believe. But the Babbitt son and daughter are
never presented to us with any portion of the conviction which
we feel about the reality of the Pulhams' George and Gladys,
a George who calls his father "boss" and a Gladys who constantly annoys and confuses her father by her apparently random
conversations until he is convinced that he has been with his
children "for altogether too long a time." Watching the children
play-acting in a parody of their parents' actions, Harry wonders
whether he and Kay really give the impression of being such
ridiculous individuals to their children. He says: "It made me see
that they did not know what we were like at all. I could
hear their voices going on around me while I sat and ate, and
my mind moved away from them."

But the great superiority of the Marquand novel to that of
Lewis is best illustrated in the understatement of the reconcilía-
tion between Harry and Kay Pulham, with Kay's "So we have
to be kind to each other, always, don't we?" We remember Kay's
sudden recognition that the truth isn't sweet, that it's rather
awful. "We're all alone. There's only you and me." And so it
was. *Babbitt,* on the other hand, is resolved, and reconciliation
between husband and wife is achieved by means of one of the
commonest and most obvious devices of popular magazine
fiction—the emergency operation, the wife's abject fear. "She
said patiently, like a cowed child, 'I'm afraid—to go into the
dark, all alone!' Maturity was wiped from her eyes: they were
terrified. 'Will you stay with me?'" George Babbitt sobbed at
her bedside. "Old honey, I love you more than anything in the
world!" To his assurance that he has been away but that now
he is back again, his wife replies:

"Are you really? George, I was thinking, lying here, maybe it would be a good thing if I just *went*. I was wondering if anybody really needed me. Or wanted me. I was wondering what was the use of my living. I've been getting so stupid and ugly—"

"Why, you old humbug! Fishing for compliments when I ought to be packing your bag! Me, sure, I'm young and handsome and a regular village cut-up and—" He could not go on. He sobbed again; and in muttered incoherencies they found each other.[6]

Enroute to the hospital George Babbitt burns his finger on the radiator in the ambulance, and it is he who ends by being consoled; she "kissed the place to make it well, and though he tried to be gruff and mature, he yielded to her and was glad to be babied."

To object to the soft writing, the "muttered incoherencies," the reversal of the situation with the consoler being consoled, is not to say that the actions described are necessarily inconsistent with the character types presented in George and Myra Babbit. It is simply that such a conclusion shows up clearly not only the thinness of texture but also the writer's recognition of a need to recapture the reader's indulgent sympathy for a character toward whom the reader has come to feel an increasing indifference. Myra Babbitt has never appeared convincing in the course of the novel, and Babbitt himself has been sustained largely by the author's extraordinary gift for a dialogue that satirizes through caricature. When there is no place else for the characters to go, and there is no possible resolution, or revelation of ultimate meaning to be derived from the characters, a slight-of-hand trick is introduced to persuade the reader, through a shift of tone from the satiric to the sentimental, that his characters have not simply dissolved into nothingness. It is not "the truth" and neither is it "rather awful," as Kay Pulham recognizes it is when she apprehends that they are all alone, that there is only the two of them.

Lewis missed the poignancy which Marquand captured. But then, he was never a novelist of marriage, or of love in marriage, as was Marquand. Lewis' novel is rounded off, the tale is told, and we remember it, if at all, for qualities quite different from those to be found in the work of Marquand. There is really no end to *Pulham*; despite the patterns of the society which shape the novel and give it its place in time, there can be no final and eternal resolution. Such is the human condition. There is always something of sadness in victory and a portion of glory in defeat. The note of tentativeness remains. A Marquand novel thus might well end with these words: To be continued, in your life—or mine. . . .

CHAPTER 5

"We're just poor boys (and girls) trying to get along"

I *So Little Time*

NOT ALL of Marquand's characters nor all of his books are concerned with the lives of patricians like George Apley and H. M. Pulham—if such they may be called. Many of his characters are not to the manor born—or, if they have memories of the manor, they were reared on the far side of the tracks. And this fact represents a side of Marquand himself. For, like the protagonists of *So Little Time, Melville Goodwin U.S.A., Sincerely, Willis Wayde,* and (to some extent) *Women and Thomas Harrow,* Marquand was one who made good even though he had to overcome obstacles and handicaps to do so. As a son of an improvident father who was nonetheless a scion of a prominent family, Marquand went to Newburyport High School instead of an exclusive prep school; there was no St. Swithin's in his background and no headmaster like "the Skipper" of *H. M. Pulham, Esquire.*[1] Perhaps for these reasons Marquand could understand and sympathize with both the patrician and the *arriviste*; for he was both—and neither.

Newburyport, the American small town, whether in New England or elsewhere, saw the genesis of many of his protagonists. Marquand called the town Clyde on one occasion. But in *So Little Time* it is Bragg, Massachusetts, where the Wilsons lived in an old house on Lime Street and Jeffrey shared a room on the third floor with Alf, his worldly older brother who knew all the latest songs and slang and had a way with the "chicks." There lived also his older sister Ethel, and his Aunt Martha and the Old Man. There were his Aunt Mary and his Grandpa, who agreed to put him through Harvard College as his graduation present from Bragg High, provided he worked summers at the carpet factory to help out. After all, he had been salutatorian of his class, and the opportunity which he was to receive was a privilege that neither his older brother nor sister had been given.

The girls of his class had faces "fresh and shining, because even a touch of rouge meant, then, that you were not a nice girl." And the boys of his class wore high stiff collars and their hair was "plastered unnaturally to their skulls." On graduation day, after he has delivered his halting salutatorian address, he hears his classmate, Christine Blair, read the class prophecy, reporting that in the distantly future year of 1933,

> Jeff Wilson, that great orator, is known the world around. The bands play, and they wave the flags, when Jeff Wilson comes to town.
> Who helps him with his speeches I can very easily see, Her first name has Lou and Ella in it, and her last begins with B.

That, of course, would have had to be Louella Barners, and Jeff could gladly have welcomed death on that occasion. Louella was that lovely girl with the yellow hair and the beautiful gold and purple bow.

Roger Butterfield, writing a biographical sketch of Marquand in *Life* Magazine some years ago, made it possible for the reader to trace a parallel between the incident in the novel and the actual one at the time of Marquand's own graduation so many years before. The class prophecy recited by Gladys Whitson declared that Marquand's "great dictionary is a marvel to behold. A day's perusal in its depths would make a boy grow old. . . . But Miss Simpson, famed philanthropist, doth with weighty brow the lexicographer entrap with definitions wise enow. . . ." The reference is to Lillian Simpson who wrote the class ode and was the apparent model for Louella Barners of the novel. Louella in *So Little Time* is the name for Beatrice, for Laura, as in other books it has been Mary Monahan, the first of the "Annabelle Lees to drift, wraithlike, through the greater novels," as another writer has put it;[2] or it is Jessica, or Marianna, or Marvin Myles, or Polly Fulton. But always there is the girl one did not get.

Like the themes of most social novelists, Charles Brady has pointed out that

> Marquand's themes grow naturally out of his own autobiographical experience; out of the deep waters of his personal well of the past as well as out of the shallower reaches of every-

day journalistic immediacy. He was born both to the purple and to the sack-cloth within the taciturn limits of a cultural complex where poorer relatives find themselves dowered with a very special status. From this dual accident of birth proceed the twin *traumata* that provide him with his psychic wound and compensatory bow of art; he was snubbed at Harvard; and either he was jilted by a girl or—both combinations appear on the Marquand chessboard—else he did the jilting. (Thackeray's twin *traumata* were grimmer: he lost his patrimony at the gambling table, and he married a mad wife.)[3]

For Jeff Wilson, however, there is too little time. There is no point in regretting the past or in shaping the future. The events of the novel take place in the midst of the sepulchral newscaster's voice announcing gravely in the midst of blitzes and buzz bombs: "This—is London." Louella Barners belonged to a past which was as unreclaimable as one's lost innocence. And in later years it was Marianna Miller in Hollywood who could recognize with him the pastness of the past and with whom he could share a hopeless knowledge that if Madge, his wife, was not right for him, "no one is exactly right for anyone else, not ever." It was always too late to go on with anything else, too late to begin again. So far as Marianna was concerned, he realized when he faced himself honestly that if it had not been for the sepulchral "This—is London," nothing would ever have happened.

Marquand in each of his novels succeeds admirably in recapturing the spirit of time and place, in evoking the nostalgic sense of unforgettable moments frozen in time. But probably no other novel succeeds so thoroughly and poignantly in projecting the dramatic knowledge of the American on the verge of World War II who remembered the events of World War I and realized that he had been there before—that it was an agonizingly familiar old story. Marquand is not a war novelist in quite the sense that Hemingway or Dos Passos or even Cummings is. But one feels that, better than his contemporaries, he is able to recapture the spirit of a time of war and to understand the forces which promote war, making it as nearly inevitable as anything can be inevitable. He seems rather an older Fitzgerald, a Fitzgerald who had lived through and beyond the chronicling of surface social phenomena until all the fine and beautiful young men seemed no longer either so fine or so beautiful but rather older, greyer, and far more knowledgeable of the wisdom of Ecclesiastes.

Of his protagonist, Jeff Wilson, Marquand writes:

> He had read *The Enormous Room* by E. E. Cummings, which at one time he had looked upon as an intellectual's artistic whimpering, and later had grown to admire. Then there was Dos Passos, and his three maladjusted soldiers. War was no place for sensitive, social-minded intellectuals. There was *Through the Wheat* by Thomas Boyd and *The Spanish Farm* and *No More Parades* and *Chevrons* and *A Farewell to Arms*. In the late Twenties and even the early Thirties, a lot of good writers had taken a crack at it; but in his opinion the net result of their efforts added up to almost nothing. They tried to give dramatic significance to something in which significance was utterly lacking. They tried to give an interpretation to something which actually offered nothing for an artist to interpret.

No one with any artistic sense was able to do anything about a war, he declares. *So Little Time* suggests that there is little that anyone can do about a war, once the voices are raised and the dumb impulsion begins to shape the course which an entire nation is to follow—however indifferent to the fact the populace may be.

The imminence of war in *So Little Time* provides the sense of crisis necessary for Jeff Wilson to engage in the searching re-examination of the past which had shaped the course of his life. In each of the novels there is such a moment of crisis resulting in the backward glance over traveled roads—the class reunion of *Pulham*, financial disaster in *Women and Thomas Harrow*, the *Time*-style interview of the General in *Melville Goodwin, U.S.A.* In each of the novels, as Alfred Kazin has pointed out, the obsessive image "is that of traveling the American road to the point of no return, to the hour when there is so little time."[4] Mr. Kazin was writing of Marquand's last book, *Women and Thomas Harrow*, but the obsession is present as strongly in all the earlier novels of the 1940's and the 1950's. The concern with the problem of change is always there. Thomas Harrow's first wife in Marquand's final novel echoes the troubled words of Harry Pulham's father when she says, "I like things so I know where they'll be tomorrow."

The fear of change takes many forms in a Marquand novel: it may take the form of greed; of dread of separation; of dread of knowledge of self; or, very often, of a kind of cultural piety manifested by a clinging to old tradition, old houses, and old values. "What bothers John P. Marquand," Kazin truly recognizes, ". . . is the suspicion that as people get older in America, they do not get wiser; they just reminisce."[5]

Of course, the flash-back is always there as the unmistakeably recognizable feature at the heart of every Marquand novel. And it was handled in his work with great skill and subtlety. Kazin's point (I believe an arguable one) is simply that the social novelist "must not exploit the fluency of his manner to describe a purely personal crisis." Kazin is quite correct in asserting that the tradition in American literature has largely been shaped by the theoreticians and the visionaries, by the Melvillian "Isolatoes" and the Ishmaels. Marquand, Kazin proposes, "writes about a society which does not want to be a society, one in which individuals distrust the very idea of society, in which social distinctions are considered immoral or irrelevant. . . ."[6] We do not care to have a Jane Austen novel sound like *Wuthering Heights,* he declares. Indeed, we do not; but Kazin recognizes, at least implicitly, that Marquand, as a social novelist writing in the first half of the twentieth century, could not be the same kind of social novelist as was Jane Austen, even if he had so desired.

It is probably quite impossible today for the social novelist, for a Marquand or an O'Hara, to avoid a sense of involvement in his society, to cultivate the degree of objective detachment which Marquand accomplished in *The Late George Apley* and which, accordingly, Mr. Kazin regards as Marquand's finest achievement. The truth is that the "purely personal crisis" which is reflected in Marquand's novels grows from the inevitable sense of participation on the part of the individual in that society. The whole point of such a Marquand novel is that the individual cannot escape the increasing awareness of his share in what Kazin himself calls "the American failure." All one can do is to cultivate the pieties, cling fast by an act of faith to the humanistic values, and resist despair by the acceptance of that stoicism which becomes increasingly marked in the Marquand protagonists. Certainly a Jane Austen would never have used titles like *So Little Time* or *Point of No Return;* but then neither could she have been aware in her world of the despairing sense of change which has been increasingly accelerated in the work of Marquand.

[88]

"We're just poor boys (and girls) trying to get along"

One critic has pointed out that Marquand's characters in the early novels were able to retreat to Boston, but with the war years even that solace is lost as the Jeff Wilsons attempt to enter "New York's aristocracy of talent, where a snobbery of energy and popular success replaces the older one of background and manners." There is a certain truth in the observation, pointing up once more that Marquand is something more than a chronicler of the Apleys of New England.

Marquand's point in *So Little Time* seems simply to be that there is no retreat anywhere in time of war, and certainly not in Boston. Butterfield, who wrote his *Life* article in 1944, asserts that at that time Marquand was as frankly puzzled by the state of the world as any of his characters were. Throughout *So Little Time* Jeff Wilson asks the question of anyone who might give him an answer: "What's it all about?" Even his wife Madge, who often seems so thoroughly remote from current reality, urges him not to worry about the war. "You can't do anything about it," she says. And he had to admire that ability of hers to turn her back upon anything unpleasant.

Faced by the greatest threat to civilization which the world had ever known, men and women everywhere seemed determined to put behind them the personal implications of their position. Jeff Wilson thought of all the luncheon clubs across America gathered in the bonds of fellowship—the Lions and the Elks, "the Brotherhoods of Redmen and American Legion Posts, and Daughters of the Revolution, and Daughters of Rebecca"—all eating the same kind of creamed chicken with peas and the cold mashed potatoes. "Why were they all together?" he asked himself. "Was there some comfort in doing the same thing? There must have been some comfort. They must have felt vaguely what he was feeling, a need for companionship, because they were moving into a grim uncharted future without their own volition, and because together there was some futile hope that they might find some solution." The Marquand conclusion, echoed with increasing certainty in the books which follow, is that "they would never find it, but they would meet and try again."

Perhaps because of the period in which it was written, *So Little Time* is certainly as filled with fear and despair and a mounting sense of urgency as any other creation of the era. Marquand's constantly reiterated question, expressed in the words of his protagonist, "What is it all about?", never finds a satisfactory answer. At the end Jeff Wilson can only express the knowledge of change, knowing that it was everywhere about him though he cannot see it. "He was thinking of what was permanent, and he was thinking that very little was, except perhaps personal relationships, but even these kept changing."

Jeffrey Wilson, a play-doctor who can successfully prepare other men's plays for the theatre but cannot create one of his own, recalls on the eve of Pearl Harbor the meaning of all the events in his life which have carried him from a small Massachusetts town, through one war, into marriage with a woman of good family, into parenthood and material success, and finally now to the verge of another war when once more he feels that there is too little time. All the change has left him no single value that is permanent. A flyer in the first war, he always felt each time he returned from a flight that he did not have much time left. It was not so much fear, he concludes, as the conviction that he would be cheated if he did not use his time fully. Now, awaiting the nation's almost inevitable participation in another war, he wonders if he was not cheated after all, whether time has not crept past him leaving him little or nothing to show for the effort expended in giving his life some significant meaning or pattern. And now he is confronted with the recognition that his own son Jim has so little time.

"I've been thinking we're pretty close to the end of the world," Jeffrey Wilson tells his wife on one occasion when she asks him to speak aloud his thoughts. Nothing will be the same when the war is over, he feels; but he knows that she doesn't really believe it. It was one of the difficulties. No one seemed able to talk with anyone, despite the fellowship and the luncheon clubs and the cocktail parties.

It was a time, the period just before the war, when worried men hung upon the words of foreign correspondents, those modern oracles who could bring reassurance or predict doom. In the 1920's, Jeffrey Wilson reflected, it had been the bankers and captains of industry, celebrated in the pages of the *American Magazine*, who had been the objects of hero-worship. Then for a time in the 1930's it had been the men of science, *The Microbe Hunters* and *The Hunger Fighters*. Finally, as the international situation had worsened and worried questions began to be asked about all the political ferment abroad, it was the turn of the foreign correspondents, men with a quality of perspicuity exceeding that of ordinary men. They hobnobbed with the rulers of all lands, took their readers inside, as it were—inside Europe, inside Asia, inside the latest crisis looming on every political horizon.

In each of Marquand's books there is at least one brilliant satirical set piece, one scathingly ironic analysis of an American type who, individualized in a character, has "made good" in the modern sense, almost in spite of himself. That figure in *So Little Time* is the foreign correspondent Walter Newcombe. Walter, one critic has asserted, is a fool. Indeed, Walter calls himself a fool. Yet that is not Marquand's final evaluation of this character. Unlike a book by Marquand, in which all the pieces fit together only on the last page, Walter Newcombe is regarded by Jeff Wilson as a man who is like a book "which contained everything in the first chapter—there might be more pages, but the first chapter was all you needed." The statement is only partly true. Walter Newcombe regards himself as a fool, but he is also a man who shows up in the course of the novel as one who is dedicated to the role into which he has been thrust by circumstance. It is one of the ironies of Marquand's world-view that Newcombe, a man who came from the same town as Jeff Wilson, and from even farther down the track, lives up to the role in which the irrational modern world has cast him. He knows no more than any of the persons for whom he writes his Tiresian prophecies of the ultimate outcome of the drama of our times. Again, Marquand delivers a tentative judgment for us regarding Walter Newcombe. The correspondent's wife, one of Marquand's better creations, recognizes him as a lovable little man who has all the human frailties but who makes up for them by his seriousness of purpose and his dedication to the cause which he has espoused as a spokesman for America and the American press.

Anyway, Walter Newcombe, as a character created by a talented novelist, is a memorable figure. When he and Jeffrey Wilson meet years later after their days in Bragg, Massachusetts, the former proudly recalls that they are the only two citizens of the small Massachusetts town who both appear in *Who's Who*. Walter is the sort of chap who went to Dartmouth instead of Harvard and who did not learn about much of anything until he became a correspondent—an obvious Marquandian thrust at colleges which educate quite as well as the Harvard he attended. Walter tells Jeff on one occasion that he has just picked up a most unusual book at the corner drugstore: Tolstoy's *War and Peace*. "I just happened to run into it," Walter said, "at Liggett's Drug Store—just before I was hopping the train to lecture at

Rochester. . . . That book weighs about a ton, but I couldn't put it down. . . ." Walter goes on to declare that "more people ought to know about that book." He wonders where it has been all these years. Yet Marquand does not seriously satirize Walter's ignorance. He does not satirize because he appears to recognize that there are too many earnest, conscientious individuals who do not know that there are other troubled people everywhere.

As the omniscient spokesman for his age, as a symbol of the certitude which all about him seek, Walter is indeed a thin and fragile reed. It is the blind leading the blind. Yet he does the best he can, poorly qualified as he is, to accept conscientiously the role assigned him. Jeffrey notes that wherever the Newcombes appear, in their Waldorf Tower suite or in the fantastic Hollywood hostelry known as The Val Halla, there is always the sense of impermanence; five minutes after their departure any trace of their presence seems to have been erased. Walter is always going away, always taking a fresh look at the situation in Europe or in Asia, always coining new phrases of hope and faith and confidence for the troubled minds of his contemporaries who turn to him for reassurance in the presence of forces which none can understand.

Marquand's gift for believable dialogue, always remarkable, is superb as he uses it in *So Little Time* to characterize the simple, earnest Walter and the harshly bitter quality of the love that Mrs. Newcombe feels for her husband:

> "I'll cable you from Hong Kong," Walter said. "I don't know about Chungking, but you'll hear from me from Calcutta, sweet."
> "WELL AND HAPPY," Mrs. Newcombe said. "LOVE TO EDWINA. Nuts."
> Walter snapped his fingers again.
> "Don't forget Edwina's teeth," he said. "The bands need tightening, sweet."
> "Keep your mind on your stomach," Mrs. Newcombe said.
> "Sweet," Walter said. "I'll tell you something. When I get back—I've got an idea. We'll buy a little farm in Connecticut, where we can be quiet, sweet.
> "That's a swell idea," Mrs. Newcombe said, "lovely, lovely, lovely."

When Walter had gone, Jeffrey stayed behind a moment.

> "You know," Mrs. Newcombe said, and she stopped, still staring at the door. "You know, he's a brave little guy."

[92]

"Yes," Jeffrey said, and he stopped too. "Yes, he's brave."
And then Mrs. Newcombe began to cry.

Walter, in becoming a celebrity, had thrust behind him the awkward days of the past when he had been "a thin blond boy with irregular teeth and incorrect posture," when his nose "always had a red shiny look, and he wore steel-rimmed spectacles." But there was a certain identification between Walter and Jeffrey Wilson, even though the latter was not a "West-Ender" like Walter and had a status almost equivalent to that of Louella Barners who lived on Center Street. Jeffrey had been to Harvard, to be sure, but his anonymous status there was best forgotten. He decides later that he was "one of those boys to whom others referred as greaseballs, or other less printable names." He was forced to confess to Louella Barners when he was home from college for vacation that he wasn't likely to have known any of the boys who had attended her senior prom unless their names started with the letter "W." He had to remind her that it was a pretty big class at college. Jeffrey Wilson's experience was not unlike that of Marquand himself, who entertained mixed emotions about his years at Harvard, as he confessed in his Twenty-fifth anniversary report: "I have brought away from it a number of frustrations and illusions which have handicapped me throughout most of my life."

Later, many years later, when Jeffrey Wilson meets Walter Newcombe once more, he wonders if the triumphant glow, the aura of success which seems to hover over Walter is not the principal solace for the half-forgotten slights and humiliations suffered in a remote past. "When you thought of it in those terms," Jeffrey concludes, "Walter Newcombe might be egregious, but not preposterous. You could imagine him carrying his past with him through every change of scene seeking blindly for some personal sort of vindication." Jeffrey Wilson could imagine it, and so, no doubt, could John P. Marquand. Jeffrey Wilson and Walter Newcombe were the poor boys who made good, who had left Bragg, Massachusetts, behind them but who could not help wondering from time to time—at least, Jeffrey Wilson couldn't—what life would have been like had they not left Bragg. Had Jeffrey, for example, married Louella Barners instead of Madge with her personal fortune and her so-secure status, he would have been "one of the men who went with their wives to the Federation of Women's Clubs' convention at Los Angeles,"

since Louella had become president of the Woman's Club of
Bragg. That was natural enough; her mother had been president
before her. She had kept up on the new books and had read the
Grapes of Wrath, which her father wouldn't have allowed in the
house. Louella could assert gravely that "times keep changing";
and Jeffrey Wilson, visiting her on the one occasion of his
return home, agreed that they did, though he wished that they
wouldn't change so fast.

She invited him back, but he never returned. "Now that
you've found your way," she said. To Jeff the words had a
solemn sound "because you never found your way. You fell into
it, or someone kicked you into it, but you never found it." That
was the way it had been with his service overseas and with his
meeting Minot Roberts through whom, in turn, he met Madge.
And then all the rest of it followed: the children, the house in
the country which Madge bought with "her" money, and dinner
at the Clinton Club, to which he could never belong himself
but where he went as the guest of his friend Minot Roberts.

Minot Roberts is the patrician of *So Little Time*. He is, declares
Charles Brady, "the fullest-blooded Stuart in his gallery; Roberts'
fleshtints have a positive port wine hue among the sparer
Marquand characters."[7] Jeffrey Wilson, the *arriviste* who marries
out of his class, recognizes, however, the book of rules by which
people like Minot Roberts live without ever having to stop to
analyze them. The rules proclaim that one is loyal to his friends,
so it doesn't particularly matter to Jeff Wilson that Minot Roberts
knows about his relationship with the Hollywood actress
Marianna Miller. He couldn't even mind when Minot made good-
natured fun of him with his mock-serious: "Don't make fun of
us; we're just poor boys trying to get along."

But it seemed obvious enough to Marquand's protagonist that,
for better or for worse, one was really kicked, or one fell, into
his fate. After the direction had been given to his life and he
had followed the road that he was to travel, there was little
point in seeking to reverse his course. When Madge, after years
of marriage, asks him: "You're not sorry, are you?" there is only
one answer, for there is no possibility of another.

"I mean," she said, "you've liked it, haven't you? The children
and the country and being here in the winter. You have liked it,
haven't you?"

You would think that everything was settled, and then when
you least expected it, a question like that would come out of

nowhere. He could not imagine why she had selected such a time to ask him.

"Why, of course I like it," he said. "Why, Madge, if you hadn't married me, I'd have been a Bohemian."

"I just sometimes wonder," she said.

"If I've said anything," he began, "to make you think—"

"No," she said, "I just wonder sometimes, if it's what you really wanted. Jeff, we *have* had a good time, haven't we?"

Nothing had changed, yet everything had changed. Speaking of his fame, Walter Newcombe once said to Jeffrey Wilson: "I just want you to understand none of this—this fanfare makes any difference. I'm just the same as I always was." Jeff replies, a little sadly, "Don't say that again. No one's the same as he always was."

No one is and no thing is. Madge's friends, Fred and Becky, represent those who attempt to cling artificially to a past which they have never known. Fred and Becky are among Marquand's better satirical portraits, with their farm and its Norman tower on the reconstructed house and Becky wearing her full pleated gingham dress and the "weeding teams" in the fields, followed by juleps on the terrace. The establishment was a bit like Jeff's comparison of Wilder's *Our Town* to a sweet potato immersed in a glass of water: "Sprouts would come from the top of it, and roots would drop down from below, seeking vainly for the earth. He might be wrong, but he thought that the play had lacked earth, except for the graveyard scene, and you couldn't do much to a graveyard. The village green had been more like that, an artistic conception more than a place." And that exactly described Fred's and Becky's place. It would have been all right—or once it might have been. But Jeffrey had the feeling that they were all dead, or taking part in charades. Always at the back of his mind was the voice of doom pronouncing, "This— is London." And for the first time—after voting for Mr. Hoover and then for Mr. Landon—Fred and Becky decided together that they must vote for Mr. Roosevelt, because, well, "because England wants us to have Mr. Roosevelt. That's the least we can do for England." The least, indeed; and perhaps, almost all things considered, the most.

Jeffrey Wilson may not be the most memorable of Marquand's characters, and for some readers the significance of *So Little Time* may seem less discernible than that of several other Marquand novels. But it must surely seem one of the truest and most personal for anyone who lived as an adult through the years immediately preceding World War II. It may be, as Charles Brady has asserted, Marquand's "richest and most ambitious novel" up to that time, though we disagree with Brady that "the topicality clogs a little. . . ." And is it, indeed, "too cluttered, too rich, too pell-mell?"[8] It hardly seems so when we reread it years later as we confront new crises and are divided by similar doubts and uncertainties.

Perhaps there could be, and can be, no final resolution to the problems which Jeffrey Wilson confronted in the years before World War II. He had found a kind of happiness with Marianna Miller, and yet his failure to be what he might have been—to be something more than a good play-doctor and a creative individual himself—was the result of all the days and years which had shaped the inescapable pattern. Ten years ago, he told himself, it might have been different, but now there was nothing which was permanent, unless it was Madge—unless it was, as Henry Pulham realized, the knowledge that passion and wish could not prevail over the days and years. The reader can assent to Jeffrey Wilson's declaration that "wars were all the same and that he was living in history, and he wished to God that he were not." Only for a moment does he escape from history and that inexorable sense of time, a not quite convincing moment as Marquand seeks to resolve the unresolvable. He places Jeff in New York's St. Patrick's Cathedral where he has gone for a moment of quiet meditation; he is unable to pray, however, after Madge and Minot Roberts have managed to get Jim into the army, thus taking, as he believes, his son from his protection. There, on Fifth Avenue, as earlier at Chartres Cathedral, he felt no sense of time. "Although the scent of incense and the burning wax from all the candles spoke of time, still time did not disturb him." He tried to pray, as he had on occasion in the Episcopal service, "Forgive us our trespasses," but the words came out as he remembered them from his youth, "Forgive us our debts, as we forgive our debtors."

II   *Repent in Haste*

The war years were disturbing ones for Marquand when, more than ever before, he began to question the traditional values which he had always accepted. *So Little Time*, the most tentative in its judgments of all the books up to this time, is followed by a slight and inferior war novel titled *Repent in Haste*. After it came *B. F.'s Daughter* (*Polly Fulton* in the English edition), which also reveals the effects of the war upon Marquand as a writer but does not advance Marquand's status as a novelist. In these two novels Marquand stands still. Always the "old pro," he could never write a *really* bad book; but he could, and did, write thin ones—almost as though he was playing the skillful Marquandian melody with a single hand.

Repent in Haste, the slighter of the two novels, shows Marquand concerned once more with the inexorable sense of time. He has reversed the familiar proverb; there is no longer time to repent at leisure. Time's wingéd chariot is making itself heard at his back; and, when he wrote, no one could know what tomorrow would bring. In all of his novels Marquand was concerned with the preservation of values which enable the individual to save himself from the flux; in the midst of change which seemed to challenge all values, he sought to find and isolate those values which made man man. In *Repent in Haste* he is asking himself questions about the nature of heroism. He is not content to see the heroic ideal lost or disavowed by modern man—or by the novelist speaking for modern man. He clings, rather despairingly to be sure, to the hope that men may discover, almost in spite of themselves, the value of sacrifice for a worthy cause, for the heroic ideal. He was never able to escape the heroic and romantic values of his popular fiction written in the 1920's; and in *Repent in Haste* he wonders, as a correspondent overseas himself, what makes the young lieutenants like Jimmy Boyden become heroes in spite of themselves. He tries to look into the middle-class backgrounds of young men who win all the crosses and medals and to see why they are what they are. The situation presented in the novel is a highly significant one; had it been developed at full length it might well have been an acutely perceptive one. But Marquand, perhaps too deeply involved in the issues himself, never quite comes to grips with the theme.

Jimmy Boyden, the protagonist of this short novel and a young flyer stationed in the Pacific area, reflects that "it's funny the way things happen . . . when there's a war on." Marquand set out to document the point and, rather obviously in the context of the novel, to seek some answers for himself to the questions that everywhere confronted him in wartime. Though certainly anything but a major Marquand novel, *Repent in Haste* proves highly interesting as a transitional work, for the reader becomes aware that the Marquand character desperately needs to find some values to replace those of the past which seemed doomed by the world cataclysm. Perhaps, too, it may be suggested that the standards and values by which earlier Marquand characters had sustained themselves were now doomed. The Jimmy Boyden of this novel has neither the small-town origin of the Jeffrey Wilsons and the Charles Greys nor the patrician background of the Apleys or the Pulhams. Back home he had lived in East Orange (or was it West Orange?), the son of a minor executive "with an annual income of perhaps eight thousand dollars," in a middle-class neighborhood and in a house with its "anti-macassars on the parlor chairs," its radio with "Jacobean legs and an inlaid front," its gas stove which "would cook without watching," and its automatic electric toaster and electric per-colator in the breakfast nook. The glass-covered bookcase in the parlor contained a set of Conrad, given to his mother as a wedding gift by the girls in the office, *Specimens of Famous Oratory,* and, of course, some of his father's college text books.

All of this, young Lieutenant Boyden had spoken of from time to time in his meetings overseas with the middle-aged correspondent named William Briggs, who had gone to Dartmouth just about the time Jimmy Boyden was being given his first nursing bottle. Jimmy had also gone to college on the money his father had put away in an insurance fund, but he hadn't had much time for studies or for concern with what "Krauts and Frogs and Wops and sharecroppers were doing." He'd been too busy learning about ways of telling a "real Joe from a drip, for instance, and how far you could go with a certain type of girl."

And so the question which middle-aged William Briggs—and perhaps middle-aged John P. Marquand—asks himself is this: "What sort of faith did Boyden and those others like him have that made them brave? It must have been something more than the valor of sheer ignorance, and more than pride, or competi-tion, or loyalty to a group. Somewhere there was some meaning in this meaningless mess that escaped all definition." The ques-tion became all the more significant when Briggs understood that they must be dying bravely, day after day, for something. The novel attempts to identify that "something." For in Jimmy Boyden, Marquand has created a character who is about as devoid of a sense of tradition or of inherited values as it would be possible to conceive.

If the Jimmy Boydens represent the future, then what kind of future could it possibly be with nothing surviving from the past which a middle-aged correspondent could recognize as familiar? Marquand, of course, is raising the question so often asked during the war years by thoughtful people concerned with ultimate national purpose. But the question means something more to him as a novelist and as a man as frankly baffled by the state of the world as his characters. He must have realized that, if he were to continue as a creative individual and an observant commentator upon the society and the manners of the postwar era, he would have to discover some standard of value capable of informing and providing a pattern for the world into which we were moving.

That standard and that pattern Marquand sought amongst the young men fighting and dying in a global conflict and, while living, experiencing years in terms of minutes. When William Briggs raises the question of what they are fighting for, young Boyden, unable or unwilling to consider abstract questions at the time, can only reply, "What the hell else is there to do? We're in here pitching, aren't we? You get used to it, Pop. What else is there to do?" And when Briggs presses for some other answer, Boyden can only insist upon his answer: "You wouldn't let the gang down, would you? That's the word—don't let down the gang."

In his last book, the rambling series of reminiscences devoted to a Newburyport eccentric out of the past entitled *Timothy Dexter, Revisited*, Marquand asserts that "environment is more interesting than the man." Whether we are likely to agree or not with this statement, the richest of Marquand's novels do grow from his re-creation of a familiar and nostalgically remembered environment from which his characters emerge to create their lives in the modern world. But environment is almost nonexistent in the case of Jimmy Boyden; or, rather, it is so poor and thin that it can hardly hold the reader's interest or enlist his sympathy and understanding. The war is the only environment which really matters so far as the young lieutenant is concerned, and it alone seems responsible for shaping the man and giving him whatever standards and pragmatic principles by which his life is conducted.

Repent in Haste has little of the Marquand flavor for this very reason. And yet it is almost pathetically painful in its attempt to understand the Jimmy Boydens of the world, who, fighting and dying for their country, have almost no life stories and who are the "consequences of a few natural impulses and a few automatic responses and other impulses." For, with such an unpromising background, the correspondent Briggs reminds himself, the lieutenant was still entitled to wear, if he wished, the ribbons representing all the citations. There was no escaping the fact that "if he [Boyden] still thought about the war as an athletic event, he was winning all the cups. . . ."

When Briggs returns to the States, he naturally visits Lieutenant Boyden's family and the young wife whom he had married after meeting her on a twenty-four hour leave—since there was so little time. The family is keeping the baby born to Jimmy and Daisy, and Daisy has another lover. Briggs tries to understand, but Daisy is quite as inarticulate as the young man she married; to her ". . . life is a sort of a rat-race, isn't it?". And Briggs, the inquiring intelligence from Dartmouth, finds himself forced to agree. "You can't help what life makes you, can you?" she asks again. When Briggs returns to the Pacific with the responsibility of telling the young husband that his wife doesn't love him anymore and has accepted another lover, he fears the consequence. Daisy has told him that one can't stay still; "he used to be a sweet kid. I guess I've got to have someone around loving me the way he did. Some girls are made that way." Or "You can't tell what's going to happen when you get married in a war" is the wisdom of Daisy, and it is a judgment concurred in by her young husband when Briggs returns to the Pacific with his information.

War was a monotony, a repetition of the same anecdotes, and this was one of them. Briggs concludes that perhaps the inarticulate young lieutenant is really older than he. At least, Boyden has the ability and the understanding to adjust to circumstances, to roll with punches, to accept every value as entirely relative in the midst of war. When the correspondent finally reveals Daisy's infidelity, he is comforted when he had come to comfort. "'You're a good guy, Pops,'" says the lieutenant, "'but don't be too hard on Daisy. Poor kid. If I had been around——.' Boyden shook his head, 'but I wasn't around. Poor kid. . . . Just remember it's happening all the time. Kids get mixed up in a war, I guess—particularly around an airstrip. It's in the atmosphere, I guess.'" Lieutenant Boyden says that too much keeps happening all the time. "They run you ragged in this war." Finally he invites the correspondent to meet the new "chick" who showed up at the USO yesterday. "She's really a cute trick," says Lieutenant Boyden. "It's funny the way things happen, isn't it, when there's a war on?"

III   *B. F.'s Daughter*

Marquand once observed that reviewers had rather missed the point of *B. F.'s Daughter*. Insofar as the observation pertains to the mood of the book, there is no doubt some basis for his complaint. Again, as in *So Little Time* and *Repent in Haste*, the writer is concerned with the collection of fragments to shore against our ruins. The point of *B. F.'s Daughter*, as Marquand saw it, lay in the mood, the recurring frustrations of the period of war, touching and affecting every life and requiring constant shift of perspective. The mood was reflected incompletely, and imperfectly, in the shift of perspective required of William Briggs, the correspondent of *Repent in Haste*, in the revaluations of value which seem to Marquand to be called for in the wartime world and in the peace which would somehow, some day, follow.

Polly Fulton expresses the thought in the confession which she permits herself at the bedside of her stricken father. "It's just as though nothing that used to count counts now," she says. "All those things you did and thought—they don't keep two people together any more. You can't go back to them, and you know there's going to be something else, but you don't know what it is."

But it is important to Marquand to attempt to learn what that "something else" is to be. Granville Hicks, in one of the more perceptive studies of Marquand's work (and there have been, surprisingly, very few), points out that Marquand never seems clearer on the problems of values than his characters are—and that is the reason, Hicks truly observes, why Marquand cannot be considered primarily a satirist.[9] Marquand's "badgered American males," as Hicks calls them, illustrate over and over the Thoreauvian observation that "most men lead lives of quiet desperation," and, on the evidence of *B. F.'s Daughter*, some women as well.

Regardless of the sex of the protagonist, Hicks suggests that one reason for Marquand's vast following from book to book was the need of the reader (like that of the novelist himself) to discover what the values are "for which there is a current market demand." If the statement is valid, then Marquand has a significance, unequaled by any other novelist of our time, as contemporary chronicler of American life in the mid-twentieth century. If literature shapes life as often as life does literature, Marquand's great popularity from *Apley* to the end of his life may well have been the result of not only his greater sensitivity to the general and widespread sense of quiet desperation felt by a whole generation, but his ability to communicate the frustration and despair created by the requirement of constant shifts in value and moral perspective—the inability or unwillingness to accept the theological implications of the not dissimilar social analyses of T. S. Eliot and Graham Greene.

Randall Jarrell wittily recognized the place of Marquand in our time when he wrote that ". . . . it *is* romantic, miraculous almost, that Marquand should be here, straight out of *The Age of Innocence,* to observe this new age of *adjusting to one's group,* and *sharing the experience of one's generation,* and getting divorced because the president of one's corporation doesn't approve of one's wife, and all the rest of it."[10] Indeed, so sensitive is Marquand as a barometer of the social atmosphere, so keenly aware is he of the prevailing winds of social change, that he might, Jarrell suggests, be retained on an annual basis by General Motors at several thousand a year and kept around the offices for an undetermined time until he had written the Great American Business Novel. It would, of course, be the same novel he had previously written, but, Jarrell asks, what of that? "What's good enough for the rest of the country is good enough for General Motors."[11]

A similar observation was made by Leo Gurko when he declared that Marquand had broken down the barriers between fiction and life; he had made his readers see their doubts of themselves and of our civilization reflected in the novels. "The pragmatic cast of Marquand's reflections on larger issues exercises a strong attraction upon his readers."[12]

B. F.'s Daughter may not be the novel General Motors would have commissioned, but its portrait of B. F. Fulton is certainly one of the most human and sympathetic in fiction's gallery of industrial tycoons. Everybody loved B. F. As Homer J. Lovelace, president of the Bulwer Machine Company, said after he had dropped everything to fly to the stricken man's bedside, "I love him. . . . You can't help loving the old sonofabitch." He is convincingly and affectionately presented by his creator, and we are ready to believe that he is a unique, made-in-America phenomenon who really means it when he says, "As long as people have an equal chance, I don't care where they begin. That's about all there is to it. An equal chance for every American boy." The phrase is embarrassingly familiar to Polly, but she hasn't the slightest doubt that it summarizes B. F.'s basic article of faith. His standard of judgment is always whether he would consider hiring someone for his office.

Early in the book B. F. tells his daughter Polly that she is like him. "I'm not like you at all," Polly said. "If you want to know, you've always been a lesson to me in everything not to do. If you want to know, I don't know how Mother's ever stood it." Despite the denial more than four hundred pages are devoted to proving that she is, unfortunately, only too much her father's daughter.

Perhaps it is unfortunate that the novel is not primarily about B. F. Fulton (Marquand's full-scale portrait of the business-man was to be *Sincerely, Willis Wade*), for the first hundred pages are as fine as any Marquand wrote. Those scenes describ-ing the friendship and mutual understanding of *nouveau-riche* Burton Fulton and young-patrician Bob Tasmin, son of a re-spected and established family, are unforgettable. Similarly, the ambiguous feelings of shame, pride, and love of adolescent Polly Fulton toward her father result in a memorable portrait of Marquand's only female protagonist. Charles Brady, in speaking of this novel as an unsuccessful *tour de force*, points out that "for the first and only time, Marquand balances a feminine protagonist against a bifurcated deuteragonist instead of merely splitting his usual male protagonist into the customary halves: conformist and rebel; traditionalistic and *arriviste*."[13] Although Marquand was less successful with women than with men characters and for this reason critics feel this novel to be unconvincing, Marquand's decision to place B. F.'s daughter, Polly, in the foreground and to give the deuteragonist roles to Bob Tasmin and Tom Brett had its own logic. It was a time of war—and Tom in particular never lets Polly or the reader forget this fact—but Marquand's first concern was with the home front, with the kind of world that remained behind when the men went to war, and with the one which would follow the war. There was an excellent reason for placing a woman in the foreground. Men had their own activities, far removed from the world of Washington and the home front. " 'Wars are men's business,' Polly said. 'Women don't belong.' " And her friend—Bob's wife, Mildred Tasmin—wonders if that isn't perhaps the reason that men like war. She says: "It does give them a vacation from women. . . ."

The note of Vanity Fair and Ecclesiastes is heard again in this novel of wartime Washington ("If you got what you wanted, did you always want something else?"), but it is not quite the mixture as before. Critics who have tended to see a falling-off in this work, or a failure to advance in terms of technique, perhaps should have regarded the novel as the third in a trilogy of American life during the war years. Viewed in perspective, fifteen years following its first publication, *B. F.'s Daughter* must be given higher marks than have commonly been accorded it. Its presentation of the wartime moods of frustrations, disorder, and contained despair is more effective and emotionally moving than that of *So Little Time*, the first of the novels dealing with the home front. The re-creation of the period in *B. F.'s Daughter* is almost painfully precise, and anyone having lived through those years as an adult could hardly fail to nod approvingly in recognition of its fidelity, or to acknowledge the expression in it of one's own most disturbing reservations about the world which would follow the war.

Marquand communicates through dozens of brilliant sketches, vignettes, and brief characterizations, the adjustments being attempted by men and women who recognized that "everything before the war is out" and who saw the uncertainties of an unforeseeable future. With nothing to hold on to and with certitude an impossibility, Polly speaks for all those about her when she inquires of her dinner companion during an evening in Washington, "But how is it going to end? How are we going to live afterwards?" We'll live, she is advised; and if she is unhappy, she must just think of everyone else. Polly soberly concludes that probably no one has a good time during a war.

The rueful note is struck again, as in the earlier novels; and the same lyric and elegiac mood is felt in the series of flashbacks by which Marquand's characters seek to escape the time-trap, or, since escape is always found to be impossible, at least to gain understanding and self-knowledge. Polly Fulton survives by accepting the knowledge of herself as she comes to know herself, by accepting Bob Tasmin's rejection of her with his words: "'We're always alone,' he said. 'Don't forget that, Polly. Everyone is always.'" "It was very peculiar what people said to you about yourself," she finally realizes. "They might say the same thing for years without its conveying any meaning, and then all at once, for no good reason, you would have lived the truth—not heard it. Know thyself was what the Bible told you."

Looking back over the years and trying to understand the vanity of human wishes, she wonders what it was she had really wanted, and "If you got what you wanted, did you always want something else?" Earlier she had concluded that "no one ever had everything for long, and after you had it for a while it did not seem like much. You did not want it when you had it. She did have everything once, and she could have had Bob Tasmin too." Polly Fulton, wealthy and guilt-ridden daughter of industrialist B. F. Fulton, was right to do as she did by falling in love with Bob Tasmin. If she was wrong to reject him because B. F. wished so fervently for the marriage to take place, still she really had no choice because, being his daughter, she would have to dominate the man she married—just as B. F. had dominated and shaped the lives of all those about him. Perhaps she really had no choice at all, or perhaps the choice she made was necessarily wrong. She married young Tom Brett, likeable, impractical, a teacher of English at Columbia University, an ardent New Dealer who spent the war years in Washington with the Office of War Information. When she finally goes to Washington, she is able to discover with no particular difficulty that there is another woman, and that "she, Polly, had plenty of nothing, plenty of complete nothing."

The most painful discovery, however, is saved for the final moments of self-knowledge gained when her first love, Bob Tasmin, to whom she turns, reveals the shocking truth about herself. For after the break has been made, and she has surrendered her right to the other woman—after she has, as she says a little smugly to Tasmin, thrown Tom Brett "out on his pants"—she gets not sympathy but a judgment. "I'm sorry for him with you running his life. Of course that is why you married him—." She is a very dangerous girl, he tells her, because she doesn't know what she is doing or why she does it: "You have to run things, like B. F. It's all right as long as you know you're doing it, but you don't know."

Leo Gurko's summary is accurate enough when he writes that "she too, like the other figures in the Marquand gallery, realizes that you can't have everything, and, in the end, is not unwilling to take less. The ache of this yielding is confined—though never eliminated—by the discovery of her real self. Even to the earlier character, this growth of self-knowledge is the reward for giving up the achievement of everything."[14]

Of course, Polly had always had too much money, and she was going to use it to "do things" for Tom, but what he really needed, as Polly learned in the confrontation scene with "the other woman," was someone duller than herself, someone " 'who doesn't—well, keep stirred up. Someone not quite as lovely— without as many definite ambitions for him. I mean someone common. That is what he needs.' She raised her hands and dropped them gently on the table. 'Like me.' " The other woman, Winifred James, was a divorcée and the secretary in Tom Brett's office. She and Tom were both Middle Westerners. Both common, "In a nice way, I mean. . . . He needs someone he doesn't have to compete with. You're so brilliant, so charming, such a rare and lovely person, Mrs. Brett. I think you're too good for him, really. I know I'm saying this badly, but he just needs someone who loves everything he does without so many perfect standards. I do hope you know what I mean."

B. F.'s judgment of Tom had not been too dissimilar. "He's bright, but he isn't stable," B. F. had said. "I wouldn't hire him for the office." It was different, though, with Bob Tasmin who, Polly said, was really an anachronism: "He was absolutely conditioned by the time he was five." The readers of Marquand's novels have met Bob Tasmin before; he is "a gentleman unafraid," as a news commentator refers to him on one occasion. He is both bright *and* stable. He is uncompromising. Polly's unspoken comparison of Bob Tasmin with an anonymous colonel with whom she spends an evening finds the scales weighing heavily in the former's favor:

> Bob would have paid the taxi driver without calling him Buddy and telling him to keep the change. He would have spoken more quietly to the waiter, and he would not have told her that she was a lovely, lovely character. He would not have waved to other people, and he would not have tried to exhibit her; instead he would have made her feel that she was the one person he wanted to see. He would not have indulged in free lectures about love and life, and he would have been able to drink without becoming noisy, and he certainly would not have tried to play footsie under the table.

In a world where all standards have been surrendered to expediency, Bob Tasmin continues to live by the rules, as had Minot Roberts of *So Little Time*, and Harry Pulham. It is a world, Polly Fulton reflects, in which "people blurted everything out with such disregard for amenities that they talked about sex and intestines as easily as they talked abut the war." And when she finds herself close to what she knows is a "sordid, vulgar, meaningless surrender" to the colonel, she puts an end to it when she thinks of Bob Tasmin. Though she can't, she always wants to tell him that he saved her "from something worse than death, or at any rate, from something."

Not that Tasmin is a stuffed shirt, though Marquand is obviously aware of the danger that his character might be thus interpreted. He is presented as a complex figure with his own burdens to bear. When his wife refers to B. F. as such an obvious person, he reflects that much of his life had been spent in association with obvious people, and he only wished that "he were as sure of what he was doing as obvious people were. . . ." He is struck by the aptness of the remark of Milton Ouerbach, the liberal radio commentator who is Marquand's principal object for satire in this novel: "We're like fish being moved from one aquarium to another. . . . We were in one body of water, and now we're in another, but everything is moving so fast I can't remember what it used to be like. Can you remember?"

For the Ouerbachs and the Tom Bretts, Burton Fulton represented a way of life that was gone: "the idea of inheritance and possession, and all that sort of static continuity, has pretty well gone out the window." For Ouerbach it is a reason for thanking whatever gods there be; for Tasmin, only a cause for regret. That "static continuity" represents all that men had meant by tradition and integrity, balance and control. It was being bred out of the modern generation. Perhaps B. F. Fulton came close to stating the reason for the universal despair when he told Bob Tasmin: "There are a lot of people who don't do anything, that is, anything that's real. That's what troubles me, Bob. Nearly everyone gets far away from real things, and I don't know why they do." The statement perhaps reflects the interest which Marquand himself felt in the people who "do things" and accounts for the selection of his own closest friends from among industrialists rather than the literati.[15]

Burton Fulton had once told Bob Tasmin, when the latter was a boy accompanying him on a sentimental journey to the industrialist's old home town in New England, that America was a wonderful place. The "real things" of which he had spoken were involved in the activities that built America.

> Bob Tasmin would often hear other people say that it was a great place, America. He would hear them say it when they were drunk or sober, and glad or sad, and sometimes he would feel the same way without saying it, but coming from Mr. Fulton, it had its own peculiar authority.
> "It's a great place, America," Mr. Fulton said. "Any boy has a chance in America if he only sees the picture . . . if he only sees the picture."
> There had been a faint chill of autum in the air, and a cool pink sunset behind the dark, wooded hills. When Bob was older and more cynical, the words often came back . . . if you only got the picture . . . if everyone could only have had the same picture . . . but the trouble was, everyone had a different one.

And Marquand saw the sadness of it. The idea is central to all of Marquand's later novels, those of the war and the postwar period. He was seeing the atomization of American life and experience; he was chronicling the destruction of those "obvious" ideals of "obvious people," and he was testifying, sadly and often nostalgically, to the moral anarchism which Alfred Kazin has termed, in reference to Marquand's final phase, "the American failure."

The pleasure in reading Marquand—quite unlike that to be found in any other contemporary writer—comes from revisiting familiar territory in novel after novel and in sharing the nostalgic re-creation of a vanished past. It is a pleasure perhaps more keenly felt by a certain generation, preferably by that born in or before the 1920's. For Marquand brings before us the less than Roaring Twenties with a veracity unequaled by any other writer of our time, not excluding Fitzgerald. Looking back upon those days of a brave new world, Marquand himself, in a retrospective review of Fitzgerald's *This Side of Paradise,* comments rather regretfully that ". . . one wishes that one's own children behaved as sensibly and nicely as the *This Side of Paradise galére. . . .*"

The essence of Marquand's own disquiet may perhaps be found in some of Bob Tasmin's regrets, expressed in the letter to his wife written when he believes he may not return from a hazardous reconnaissance detail in the Pacific. "I don't believe until you get into a box like the one I'm in right now, you ever realize how much you have always taken for granted. First you accept day and night, and then the seasons, and then you accept a mode of existence and a whole assortment of theories and ideas. You accept them without paying too much attention exactly as you accept your friends. You fall into a groove. You only think about this when it's too late." That which is accepted without question—a mode of existence, a set of values—suffers the attrition of time until nothing of real importance remains. And this happened because one does not care enough, because one is not alive enough, because one accepts the easy compromises and forgets the past and the promises associated with it.

The truth was, as Bob Tasmin saw it, that there were too many answers for America, each supplied by a group antipathetic to every other group. "Bob would have enjoyed pointing out that Milton [Ouerbach] and his whole intellectual class were just as pompous and supercilious, as careful of prerogative and protocol, just as arrogant and as much a privileged group as the military men whom Milton disliked. The truth was that all liberals were turning into selfrighteous, complacent social snobs, and each faction was the only one that understood America." The point was, so far as Bob Tasmin was concerned, that one had to live by rules. Facing probable death on the mission he was about to undertake, he reminded himself that the Apostle's Creed, now very old-fashioned, was itself a set of rules. And as in the game of chess, "You either moved on diagonals or one square at a time, depending on what you were, but you had to live by rules."

Bob Tasmin did not question that there were things wrong with him. Or rather, the things that were wrong with him were not really wrong, as Polly Fulton said. It was just that "the things that are right with you are just too damned right."

> She used to say that he danced too well and his tennis was too good. His clothes never looked rumpled and nothing ever seemed to sag. He behaved himself when he was tight, and he was wonderful with parlor tricks—those songs of his. He was even wonderful in the broadminded, tolerant way he loved her.

He concluded that one always lived in a narrow world "from which you tried to escape in many tentative little ways, or else you burst out of it with a bang, but even if you did, you only got into another that had other limitations." Finally, the real attribute of greatness was the ability to accept charitably what one did not know. "There was only one thing you could take with you wherever you went, and that was a little knowledge."

Bob Tasmin could see himself just as Polly must have seen him—"a member of the well-stocked club group which was indigenous to the Eastern seaboard and which had a culture stemming from the British upper middle class—a group with good manners and one which had trained itself in several generations of security." But being a gentleman was not the easiest thing in the world, particularly when it meant not compromising with the standards which had been responsible for shaping one's conduct and one's life. When he is finally forced to refuse, like a gentlemanly Henry Esmond, Polly's desperate invitation to her bed, when his control commands the situation despite himself and his desires, he bursts out: "All right, . . . I've always been a goddam gentleman, and I've always been afraid not to be one. Let's put it on my tombstone. That's my whole obituary."

Or in more mundane terms, Polly realized that, in contrast to Tom Brett whom she had married, "Bob Tasmin would not be mixed up with other women. Bob Tasmin would not need sedatives for insomnia, and if he threw cigarettes at the fireplace, they would land there. His trousers would be neatly folded on a chair, and he would not leave his pajamas in a heap on the floor." And that was the way it was. That was Robert Tasmin, and that was the way it used to be, Polly liked to remind herself, in 1940 "before the war fixed it so that no one had time for anything."

CHAPTER 6

"Fate gave what chance shall not control . . ."

BUT IF the "war fixed it so that no one had time for anything," as Polly Fulton concluded; and if during those years one thought that there was going to be something else after the war—even if one didn't know what it was to be; or if war was, in one sense, a vacation from women—the years which followed were quite clearly unlike anything which the returned soldier had conceived.

Marquand gives us the picture in his first postwar book, *Point of No Return,* through the eyes of Charles Grey, who goes to the bank each morning on the commuter's train from his prewar $30,000 suburban home, the ruptured duck pinned in the buttonhole of his neat conservative suit. To get ahead in that brave, new, postwar world, there is a great deal of apple polishing to be attended to—a fact which he is never allowed to forget either by his wife Nancy or by the precariously competitive struggle for advancement in which he is engaged with Roger Blakesley, the other probable candidate for the bank's recently vacated vice-presidency. "If you had to earn your living," he decides, "life was a series of apples."

Point of No Return is a remarkably successful novel by any standard, popular or critical. It is precedent to and documentation of the innumerable theses which were to be advanced in the next dozen years by critics of American society. It contains elements, relating to suburban housing, of John Keats' *The Crack in the Picture Window;* of William H. Whyte's *The Organization Man,* in that it reflects the elements of social status and class in the business and industrial hierarchies; of David Reisman's *The Lonely Crowd;* and of a book like Margaret Halsey's *This Demi-Paradise: A Westchester Diary.* But as a picture of the

JOHN P. MARQUAND

immediate postwar era, and as one more inclusive than the
individual volumes named, *Point of No Return* is probably a
more satisfactory work for the general reader, both as art and as
a document of the times, than any of these studies. Perhaps only
two works of nonfiction have presented the period more compre-
hensively—Max Lerner's *America as a Civilization* and Eric F.
Goldman's history of the years between 1945-60, *The Crucial
Decade—And After*—and both have apparently drawn upon
novelist Marquand for numerous insights.

I   *The Varieties of Love and Success*

Charles A. Brady is representative of the many critics who
expressed a greater personal and critical preference for *Point
of No Return* than for any other of Marquand's novels. It is,
declares Mr. Brady, Marquand's "most three-dimensional novel
to date, possessing as it does his old mastery of reproduction and
criticism of life, together with a deepened power over creation
of life,"[1] particularly in relation to the secondary characters. He
observes truly that Marquand's faculty of continuous growth, as
demonstrated in this novel, sets him apart from many of his contemporaries who often fail to grow and who may even retrogress.

More than ever in this volume is Mr. Marquand the Thackerayan
novelist of personal memory, the laureate of the sick, throat-
filling, despairing ecstasy of first love. He understands the
mystery and the magic of the human personality with a mellower
comprehension than before. In the realm of the Cyprian goddess
the Marquand mixture is no different. Charles Grey loses his
first love and succeeds in his second job. But this time the
frustrate lover wears his rue with a difference. Jessica Lovell,
ghost-like, fades down the winds of memory. Man is still alone,
even in love; perhaps above all in love. Nothing is certain. But
there are compensations between the "morning that separates"
and "the evening that brings together for casual talk before the
fire." Charles Grey, for example, "felt contented and at peace
doing nothing but raking leaves on the lawn, he and his two
children."[2]

To be sure, Marquand is, in this novel, once more the novelist
of love in marriage; he is certainly, as Mr. Brady has pointed
out, the novelist of personal memory. There is "love" and there
is "being in love." It was "being in love" with Jessica Lovell,

whose ghostlike memory persists through the years; but it was "love" with the woman he married, who bore him a son and a daughter, who was always terribly efficient, and who, finally, was responsible for keeping Charles Grey on his toes and in the running for the vacated vice-presidency. For Nancy, Charles Grey felt the kind of love which, like that of Harry Pulham for his wife Kay, was not the result of "passion or wish, but days and years." Charles Grey knew Nancy Grey so well—so well that "there was no actual chance for decent concealment when you knew someone's voice as well as he did hers. It was all part of the relationship that was known as love, which was quite different from being in love because love had a larger and more embracing connotation. It was a shadowy sort of edifice built by habit, without any very good architecture, but still occasionally you could get enough impression of its form to wonder how it had been built." And the habit finally came to be everything—or almost everything. And the raking of leaves on the lawn with his two children could be both a part of the habit and one of the compensations for it at the same time.

This novel, like earlier novels of Marquand, is concerned with the nature of love, of being in love, of love in marriage; but it will surely be remembered longer for its examination of the prevailing definitions of success in mid-twentieth century America. Is the game—and it is a "game," strenuous and exhausting—worth the candle? Such is the question asked throughout; at the end the answer is: Well, maybe yes and maybe no, but on the whole, probably not. A conclusion singularly without cheer, it implicitly rejects the ethos fostered by modern business and industrial life; and this fact was apparently recognized in the very successful adaptation of the novel for Broadway production by Paul Osborne.

While approving in general of Osborne's felicitous treatment of the material, Marquand disclosed in an interview appearing in the *Saturday Review* that the play's original ending, which had adhered closely to that of the book, was changed to present Grey in a more heroically independent stance. Marquand said of Charles Grey in the book: "He sees he has passed the point of no return and might as well accept it. This ending made the play say the same thing the novel did, roughly, 'The game in many ways is not worth the candle.' But evidently the producers found the audience wouldn't take to such a pessimistic result so Osborne now has Charles Grey show a kind of revolt by refusing to join the Hawthorne Hill Country Club as the boss requests. This makes the play seem to mean 'The game may be worth the candle if you learn to walk erect.' "[3] The new ending, Marquand suggested, came as something of a shock since everything else in the play rang true and coincided with the situations presented in the book. But, he said, one had to "soup it up" to win acceptance of such a cheerless proposition in the theatre.

In preparation for the conclusion at which Marquand has his character arrive, he presents once more in the fullest and most precisely moving detail the preceding thirty-five years of American life, a period which, as Granville Hicks has declared, he knew "as unerringly as one of Mark Twain's pilots knew the Mississippi River."[4] And it is Marquand's own village of Newburyport which is undisguisedly presented as the prototype for Clyde, Charles Grey's home.

II No Turning Back

The re-tracing of these years through his habitual use of the flash-back is necessary in *Point of No Return,* just as it had been in the earlier novels, to demonstrate Marquand's most firmly held conviction that there is no turning back to the road not traveled by; that conditioning, as in the case of every Marquand hero, inevitably results in the necessity of each man's recognizing his own point of no return. This conviction, which comes as close to a philosophical idea as any feature of Marquand's work, was no doubt unsympathetically received by many of his readers who accepted the elements of the romantic tale in his novels but sought to reject his realistic treatment of his hero's submission to his destiny. Many critics, familiar with the antitraditionalistic phenomenon of revolt and rebellion in the classic American novel, find something a little too Roman in Marquand's characters; they distrust the stoicism of these protagonists, the recurring note of Ecclesiastes. Even astute critic Maxwell Geismar seems hardly to know what to make of a curious fellow like Marquand. While speaking of him as one of the "conservators of heritage," like Willa Cather or Ellen Glasgow or, he might have added, Edith Wharton, Geismar asserts in a review of *Point of No Return* that Marquand need not for that reason "sacrifice, as he does here, everything he knows about American life and expresses so well, to the demands of a sentimental and romantic tale. True enough, Charles accepts his advancement

with acrid knowledge that he has lost his freedom forever, and
this takes character. But it is character that lacks the real courage
to make the break, whose virtue is compromise, and whose
discipline is the discipline of submission."[5] It is difficult to see
how it could be both a "sentimental and romantic tale" with
such an acknowledgeably realistic conclusion. The reader may
decide for himself whether the "real courage to make a break"—
in the American novel's tradition of rebellion—or the recognition of self-knowledge and of the need for submission to order
and discipline is the romantic way.

It is a curious feature of the American novel that so many of
its major protagonists are Ishmaels—"Isolatoes," as Melville put
it, outcasts and pariahs. They do not fit the backgrounds of the
societies against which they are projected. Our literature is so
full of unquiet hearts—the Joe Christmases, the Eugene Gants,
the Jay Gatsbys, all the unatoned ones—that it must seem somewhat anomalous to many critics and readers when they come
upon submission and acceptance. After all, Billy Budd is surely
as American as Bartleby—or Lewis Lambert Strether as Frank
Cowperwood.

There is less difficulty in understanding Mr. Geismar's position on this score—in view of the stand he has taken in defense
of the novel of revolt and social protest as most characteristic
of the American tradition—than there is in explaining the attitude
which he shares with some other critics toward Marquand's treatment of the past, a treatment which he regards as sentimental
and unreal. Certainly, as he acknowledges, the "older native
scene did—and does—exist," but is it true that Marquand was
able to catch it only "through nostalgia and romance?" If the
narrative of events taking place contemporaneously is as effective
as it is commonly agreed to be, it must be recognized that a
large part of that effectiveness is achieved and heightened
through the contrapuntal effect which Marquand achieves by
his precise and firmly realistic handling of detail from that past
which has so indubitably shaped and created the patterns of
the present. We must disagree emphatically that the novelist
"loses his grip" when attempting to present in a serious situation the complexities of human character and relationships, at
least in this and earlier novels; and I shall have something more
to say upon this matter in relation to the last work of Marquand
which may seem in some degree to support Mr. Geismar's charge.

III *Competitive Life*

We are constantly impressed by what must be either an extraordinarily retentive memory for detail or the most painstaking research as we read and reread with delight Marquand's moving re-creations of the past. The truth is, for those of us who have ever lived in a small American town in the first thirty years of the twentieth century, that the nostalgia, if it is felt (and it would be almost impossible not to feel it), results from a recognition of the accuracy of the picture—a picture in which, even down to the current slang and the songs of the day, we are able to see ourselves. And we can see the meaning of Charles Grey's competition with Roger Blakesley for the vice-presidency of the conservative old Stuyvesant Bank in New York only if we have first the knowledge of the all-consuming desire of Charles Grey to win Jessica Lovell, whose father was upper-upper and had too much money for a lower-upper like Charles Grey to aspire to his daughter's hand. We must also see Malcolm Bryant, the anthropologist, who comes to Clyde for the purpose of making his famed survey of social status in a typical New England town and who saw man as always and everywhere essentially the same, "whether he's in G-strings or plus fours. . . ." It was necessary to know that Malcolm Bryant had proposed to Charles Grey, perhaps only half-seriously, that he accompany him on an expedition to the Orinoco, and to know that Charles regarded it only as a kind of escape to a region where there were no Cadillacs, "no Boston theatres, no walks like that one across the pasture, no spring sunsets above the river, and no savage chiefs more difficult to placate with beads and bangles than Mr. Laurence Lovell," Jessica's father, who could not or would not bring himself to accept the obviously serious intentions of young Mr. lower-upper-class Charles Grey toward his daughter. "All the elements of his life were moving as they should that spring," Marquand reflects regarding his young Mr. Grey, "and he did not have the sense to pray that eventual compensation should be light." He did not have the sense, in short, to recognize, as any realistic young New Englander should have recognized, the Emersonian law of compensation; that there had to be a balance and a return for his good luck, his good fortune, and his extraordinary happiness.

The compensation comes, and he loses both his first job with the brokerage firm of E. P. Rush and Company and his first love, Jessica Lovell. For in his relationship with her at this time he was "Jason back with the Golden Fleece, and at one and the same time, he was the small-town boy who had made good and the embarrassed young man who would have to speak to her father. He was also the gilded youth of the Jazz Age, in his high-powered car, and Jessica, bare-headed, in her print dress, was a part of the age too, and so was the spring evening." She was for Charles like Fitzgerald's Daisy of *Gatsby*, but much better known and a great deal more believable.

The time had to come when he was not too impressed by Jessica, when he had to face the fact that he lived on Spruce Street (lower-upper) and not Johnson Street (upper-upper). And so what of it? The time had to come, as it did so abruptly, when he faced Mr. Lovell in his daughter's presence and said he wanted to marry her. He had to accept the father's near-faint, relieved by the glass of water rushed to his lips by his daughter; and finally he had no choice but that of accepting the rambling and apologetic reminder that, after all, what could Charles do for his daughter (beyond making her happy) in the humble position which he held with E. P. Rush and Company, despite the $50,000 he had made on the market. " 'Money is one thing,' Mr. Lovell said, 'and stock-market money is another.' " Certainly it was not the same thing, Mr. Lovell said, as "inherited money." Jessie assured her father that he would get used to it in time . . . but he didn't . . . and she didn't. They might be secretly engaged, but Mr. Laurence Lovell "had not asked for it or expected it, . . . now they must share this period of strain together as best they could. They must bear and forbear and it was no time for jubilation."

Aunt Georgianna approved and promised that they should have the silver tea set. Despite Jessica's assurance that "daddy" had taken it well, Georgianna (Miss Lovell, and every New England family had to have one) remarked with foreboding that to take it well would be more than could be expected of him. As for Jessica, "it was dreadful knowing what the two people she loved most in the world must have been going through." Marquand's point is clear enough: Jessica had been as perfectly conditioned by the age of five as had Bob Tasmin of *B. F.'s Daughter*; not even love, or biology, would be strong enough, finally, to change her unalterable course.

But it was also the conditioning of Charles's father John Grey, which in the end was in large part responsible for making it all impossible. Here was a Montague-Capulet affair, with the unrevealed animosity between the families stemming from an unacknowledged social difference. John Grey, for whom everything went wrong in business, in investments, in life, wanted it understood that he should have a frank talk with Laurence Lovell the very next day since there seemed an implied insult in the fact that the engagement was not to be publicly announced. After the engagement was announced, it didn't help for father John Grey to charter a yacht for a month with his market profits; everyone laughed about it as another silly and ridiculous extravagance, even though it probably did not cost much more than a winter cruise to the Caribbean.

Later, Charles Grey reflects how it might have been had Jessica Lovell finally been something more than a ghost, but as it was he had the knowledge of a theory of time:

> If there were anything in the theory that the past remained intact, he and Jessica Lovell must still have been somewhere, with the other ghosts of Clyde. Perhaps all of that summer might have returned to him again and again if he had stayed in Clyde. If he had never seen Jessica Lovell again except in the distance, he would have seen the shadows of Jessica and himself around every corner and on every country road. If he had walked down Dock Street, he and Jessica might still have been standing in front of the window of Stowell's furniture store, talking of living room curtains. She had wanted green monk's cloth curtains. Down at the foot of Gow street, they might still have been gazing at the FOR SALE sign on the Pritchard house, for old Miss Pritchard had died that summer. It was in bad condition, but they could have fixed it up if they had bought it. If he had gone to the beach in the moonlight, he and Jessica would have been there with their picnic supper. Their two shadows would have been everywhere, because they had been everywhere in Clyde together. By God, it was a wonderful town.

During those last months of the engagement, father Lovell had remarked to Charles, when they were alone together, that it was a great shame that he had not gone to Harvard instead of Dartmouth, and Jessica always reminded him that it wasn't meant as it sounded. It did no good for Charles to remind Mr. Lovell that there were a great many good schools beside Harvard.

There was always that pressure. Jessica couldn't stand it if Charles didn't like her daddy and if her daddy didn't like Charles. They had to get to like each other. But though Charles tried, he had little opportunity to be liked in return, for neither of them "knew the art of placation." There was a difference not to be overcome in Clyde between the Lovells, who had been shipowners, and the Greys, who had been ship captains. "The Lovells had made money out of shipping while the Greys had only worried along. Yet both of them had tried."

Money! It is a theme which Marquand handles as surely as any novelist of the modern world, more obliquely, to be sure, than either Dreiser or Dos Passos, certainly more indirectly than Balzac, but its influence is always felt—nowhere more powerfully than in *Point of No Return*. When Francis Stanley, who has more money and position than Laurence Lovell himself, can suggest that there is something between Lovell's daughter and a lower-upper like Charles Grey, why, then, it is time to be concerned. Even Jessica is able to see the seriousness of the situation. Mr. Lovell can put up with only so much foolishness; however, "it does show where we have drifted" if someone like Francis Stanley ventures to congratulate him on the forthcoming marriage of his daughter to a lower-upper like Charles Grey. "It shows what other people must be saying. I don't mind about myself, Jessica, but I can't have your name becoming a byword."

Later, Charles's wife Nancy could tell him, "Pull up your socks and forget it." That was after the crash of 1929, and Charles knew that he really couldn't have done anything about the economic disaster. Everything went to pieces then, so far as the old life in Clyde and his father's self-assurance were concerned. "We can't help how we're made, can we?" his father asks; and indeed this is the point that Marquand, a son of the Enlightenment and one of its most convinced environmentalists, illustrates over and over. But for John Grey the events of October, 1929, were conclusive; an impractical man, he had never signed the papers setting up a trust fund for his wife and family.

Charles's government bonds went into the sadly depleted estate his father had left in order to make up the losses, without the knowledge of his mother and sister, for of course there was nothing else to do under the circumstances. It was the right thing to do, Jessica agreed, and they could be married anyway. But, before he left Clyde forever after father Lovell ended the romance for good, he saw her only one more time. It was then that Charles Grey learned the meaning of class and of status in America; he realized that he and his father as Spruce Streeters did not belong to the Johnson Street of the Lovells. This lesson he never forgot during the later years while he was making his way to the top in the Stuyvesant Bank.

Such was the necessary background—certainly far from our usual understanding of a romantic or sentimental tale—for the ambition and the desire to "show them"; for he and Nancy spent the years attempting "to beat the system." They were, they felt, two against the world:

> She never had to explain whom she meant by "them" or what it was they were going to show. It was always himself and Nancy against the world and against all the systems in it, against Tony Burton and the Stuyvesant Bank and American Tel & Tel, against the furnace and the doctors and the bills. It was always himself and Nancy striving for security, and they never needed anyone to help. It was always himself and Nancy, striving within the limits of free enterprise if you wanted to put it that way.

In the competitive struggle Nancy had grown just a bit sharper, more resilient, more sensitively aware of the nuances in the meanings expressed by the people who mattered and who needed to be tactfully cultivated for the purpose of their own advancement and success. Charles, too, became daily a cannier person, adept not only at the conversational style that waited to catch unconscious overtones, but at parrying the thrusts directed against their security. For he always knew, whether Nancy realized it or not, that she was really a Spruce Street girl and that, therefore, it had to be him and Nancy against the world.

When he finally returned to Clyde on business for the bank, he recalled the fantasies which he had daydreamed in the past of driving past the Lovell's house on Johnson Street and pointing it out to Nancy: " 'That's where she lived,' he would say. 'It's perfect Federalist architecture, but it's sterile, isn't it?' " Or in the air corp uniform of a lieutenant colonel he would be driven through, stopping long enough to light a cigarette before Walter's Drugstore and to have people recognize him with wondering admiration before dropping his cigarette and driving indifferently away. He had come a long way since those days in Clyde, Charles liked to remind himself.

The conclusion which he had to reach—after his visit to Clyde and his years of striving for advancement in the bank—was that while life, liberty, and the pursuit of happiness expressed sentiments which all could embrace, the more one pursued happiness the less liberty there was to be enjoyed; at least it seemed so in Charles Grey's world: ". . . if you pursued it hard enough, it might ruin you. His father had died pursuing it." One was always hurrying, but no one ever told the school children that it did little good to hurry if the only result was that one hurried to return to one's responsibility of "taking care of other people's money." Finally, the truth came home that, if it all could be done over again, one would have acted in the same way and made the same mistakes. Words to the contrary were, in his lost brother Sam's words, "Just the same old bushwa, kid."

When Charles returned to New York the following day, feeling that he had been away for ages, he could understand Nancy's words when she met him with the children and drove him home: "The first thing for you to do is to get to know the children all over again. I can come later and more gradually. We all may be a little shy with each other at first but we can all adjust together." But the gentle irony he understood. Nancy and Charley understood even if their daughter Evelyn did wonder about the turn of the conversation since, after all, "Daddy" had been away only two days. With the talk about a boat and a pony, which Charles had been promised but had never received, the Grey children realized that perhaps "Papa" would find the means after all, that "Papa" might really get the promotion to the vice-presidency about which they had indirectly heard so much.

There are no second chances in J. P. Marquand's world, any more than in the fictional world of Henry James. This recognition comes to Marquand's Charley Greys and Harry Pulhams just as surely as it does to James's Strether of *The Ambassadors*, his Dencombe of "The Middle Years," or his John Marcher of "The Beast in the Jungle"—to name only the first three of the Jamesian characters who come to mind.

But in pursuing the only course open to us, we reach the conclusion that perhaps the game is not worth the candle after all. "Contrived" is a favorite word with Marquand; it is used to express the pattern in which we find ourselves in a world shaped by the necessity for "getting ahead" but which somehow seems to lack a sense of reality. Polly Fulton had told Bob Tasmin that everything was so "contrived"—a term used by one critic to suggest what he found wrong with the book! In the opening chapter of *Point of No Return* Charles Grey, on the point of catching the commuter's train for the city, declares that the whole business of the way of life in which they play their part is like something from Tennyson—it's all so "contrived": "The little woman kissing her husband good-by. Everything depending on this moment. He must get the big job or Junior can't go to boarding school. And what about the payments on the new car? Good-by, darling, and don't come back to me without being vice-president of the trust company. That's all I mean." With one's shield or on it!—but Nancy tells him not to say that, and when he asks her why, she replies: "Because maybe you're right." At the end of the novel, Charles Grey returns to the same thought. "'Oh, God,' he said, 'I wish everything weren't so contrived.'" And when she asks him again what he means, he replies: "'I mean what I say.' He had not intended to sound so bitter. 'I mean it's all so superficial. The bank president and the big job, and what will happen to Junior, and whether a boiled shirt will help. The values of it are childish. It hasn't any values at all.'" Finally, after the word of the appointment to the vice-presidency comes to them following a dinner at the Tony Burton's, they find it all a dreary anticlimax.

After all the years of struggling to attain this seemingly unattainable but now achieved goal, Charles wondered at the little actual pleasure he felt: "He was a vice-president of the Stuyvesant Bank. It was what he had dreamed of long ago and yet it was not the true texture of early dreams. The whole thing was contrived, as he had said to Nancy, an inevitable result, a strangely hollow climax. It had obviously been written in the stars, bound to happen, and he could not have changed a line of it, being what he was, and Nancy would be pleased, but it was not what he had dreamed." Nor is it ever, in a Marquand novel, what one has dreamed, yet it is settled for: there is obviously no other course open to any man after his destiny has been shaped by all the forces which have gone into the directing of his life. The promotion had its compensations—the new country club, the sailboat, the pride which Nancy would feel—and, while Charles knew that Mr. Laurence Lovell would never have understood, Nancy would. Still, it was not "what he had dreamed."

Malcolm Bryant would also have understood—but objectively. The anthropologist who had come to Clyde years before to do research among the natives and to write a significant sociological study titled *Yankee Persepolis* had as his model sociologist-anthropologist W. Lloyd Warner, whose completed study of the Australian aborigines led him to the project of studying the "whole man" in his socio-cultural frame of reference in a modern

American community. The result was *Yankee City,* which was based upon Marquand's Newburyport (or Clyde), Massachusetts, a town of 17,000 inhabitants. As another sociologist, Joseph A. Kahl, has put it in his *The American Class Structure,* Newburyport had become in recent years only another small town not too far from Boston (and the Harvard Graduate School of Business Administration which Warner represented). Many of its younger citizens had left the small town for New York or Boston where opportunities were greater. "One such young man," Kahl writes, "was Charles Grey, hero of John P. Marquand's novel . . . for Clyde and Yankee City are the same place (and Malcolm Bryant and W. Lloyd Warner are the same man, though many people find it difficult to explain the portrait by the sitter.)"[6]

Marquand supposedly wrote a satire on the American academician in the character of Malcolm Bryant; and, to be sure, the characterization is sharp and pointed enough, representing the "pampered, preposterous creatures who lived an artificial life, who did not want to understand or be like other people." Bryant represented "the unskillful ignorance of most dwellers in ivory towers." Marquand, Granville Hicks asserts, "has a better understanding of the class structure of contemporary American society than Lloyd Warner and all his advisers, colleagues, and assistants put together."[7]

There is truth in this assertion. However, Marquand's treatment of Malcolm Bryant is not without understanding. Marquand would have been as ready to accept the conclusion that men are shaped by environmental factors—the cultural and sociological forces which create the pattern of communities—as Warner himself. Charles Grey—and no doubt Marquand as well—resented the intrusions upon privacy, the betrayal of friendship and confidence, the coldly objective and analytical appraisal of cultural patterns based upon the outsider's warm acceptance into the tribal community. "Don't forget that all men are primitive," says Malcolm Bryant to Charles Grey when they lunch together years after the study had appeared. "You ought to know that. You're primitive." And to Malcolm Bryant, or perhaps to Lloyd Warner as well, Clyde (or Newburyport) is also primitive and follows the pattern of any aboriginal community. It is a conclusion that Charles Grey is unwilling to accept, for it seems to him that people like Bryant are likely to oversimplify. Bryant's answer is that "man only has a few basic behavioristic patterns that are constantly repeated with silly variations. You can't over-simplify. That's the beauty of it."

Grey and Bryant represent a contest between the humanistic and the anti-humanistic points of view. Charles Grey has no arguments on his side; he has only his faith in the sense of achievement, in his knowledge of the meaning of aspiration. He refuses to see man without his cultural veneer. And he rejects the attribution of lower-upper status to himself in Bryant's book, even though he must finally accept it in fact, whether it be an unreasoned tribal superstition or not.

He has been described in Bryant's book as a lower-upper, who may aspire to but not under any circumstances achieve recognition by the upper-upper. Indeed, there is so much truth in the conclusion of the dweller in an ivory tower that Charles Grey can never quite overcome the popular folklore. Only after years have passed and he is on the verge of promotion to the vice-presidency of the bank, can he declare to his wife Nancy: it was all for the best. Even though his friend Jackie Mason stayed at home in Clyde, was elected to all the better clubs and made the most important associations, became en-gaged to Jessica Lovell, got ahead in Clyde and "had every-thing," Charles Grey finally has to conclude that he would do it all over again in the same way if that were possible. He can't really say it, but if he could he'd tell Nancy that they've been together so long . . . and he'd do it all over again if he had the chance.

Point of No Return has its sharp passages about anthropologists who are interested in people only academically, who treat individuals like case histories, who are interested in results rather than causes, and, perhaps equally important, who don't write very well in the first place. Yet at the same time Marquand seemed to realize that Warner had hit upon a basic reason for modern man's discontent in his alienation from the rootedness in a stable group which the Clydes (or the Newburyports) once provided. There were parallels between such towns and the primitive societies which Warner had studied—as William H. Whyte, Jr., in his *The Organization Man* has pointed out:

> It was a venerable old New England town rich in tradition and full of people with a strong attachment to the past. There were Memorial Day celebrations instead of the Nurngin totem rites, but in many ways it seemed much the same, and Warner drew the same moral. Of the many conclusions that come out of the

study, by all odds the most important finding was the function of social structure in fixing the individual in a satisfying relation to the society.[8]

The small town revisited or lost is a familiar theme in American literature; and the knowledge that in America one can't go home again wakens an echoing response in the breasts of most readers in our highly mobile society. Willa Cather's "lost lady" and Eliza Gant's "lost son" belong to the same recognizable family. "They can never really go back," Mr. Whyte declares in writing of his American "transients." "Once the cord is broken, a return carries overtones of failure." He reports one executive as saying, "I'm fed up with New York, but if I went back to Taylorston I know damned well they'd think my tail was between my legs."[9]

In America, perhaps particularly in America, we all come to recognize the "point of no return." We may regard nostalgically that past in an American town or village which was seemingly more orderly and more secure while recognizing that we can never really return to it. It is difficult, then, to understand the complaint of Maxwell Geismar that these flash-backs to small-town life in the novels of Marquand are essentially sentimental and unreal. The charge seems entirely unjustified when it is realized how the counterpointing of these passages serves to develop the basic theme of a novel like *Point of No Return*. In a reminiscence such as the following, we must recognize the symbolic implication which is present as well as the quiet charm of the narration which avoids both the sentimental and the unreal:

> They used to play hide-and-seek in the old back garden of the Meader yard in the spring, just when it was getting dusk—he and Melville Meader and Earl Wilkins and all the rest of the crowd along Spruce Street. There was a better chance of hiding, just when it was dusk. You could hide downstairs in the barn or back of the carriage shed or anywhere in the garden. There was always that indecision, that rushing about, until you heard "five hundred, coming, ready or not." Then you tried to sneak back without being seen. The best way was to dodge around the carriage house and then to the corner of the barn where you could watch the back porch, which was home, until everything was clear. There was always an uncertainty, a wondering whether you could make it, and then that dash for home. If you got there safely, all the other incidents were behind you. There was a triumphant, out-of-breath feeling, a momentary impression that nothing else mattered, when you called out "Home Free!"

It was a cry which Nancy and Charles Grey no doubt often wished they might have sung out gladly as they waited in their mortgaged house at their "point of no return" for the security which always seemed as illusory as the remembered past. In the world of Sycamore Park, the Stuyvesant Bank, and the Oak Knoll Country Club there was no place to hide at dusk, there was no "triumphant, out-of-breath feeling" in success, and there was no sense of being "home free." "Fate gave, what chance shall not control. . . ." Matthew Arnold's words remain for the Greys their unspoken conclusion.

CHAPTER 7

There's Something About a Soldier

THE PROFESSIONAL SOLDIER, a fascinating figure to Marquand, was one about whom he apparently had great difficulty making up his mind. As we have already noted, generals and officers of the regular army appear frequently in his work, and Marquand develops something like a pattern representing the changing attitudes through the years of peace and war on the part of the civilian toward these men whose lives are devoted to defense of their country. One of Marquand's first short stories —or at least one of the earliest which he chose to preserve—"Good Morning, Major," takes up the subject of the professional soldier, and the impression is not a favorable one. Generals of an earlier age, he comments in a note to the story, "were apt to be rougher around the edges and more arrogant than their 1940 counterparts." But Marquand himself could hardly decide in the years of peace precisely what he thought. Even during the war years he suggests that officers of the highest rank are rather stuffy, unimaginative, and lacking in humor. Listened to with the attention once accorded priests, they nevertheless appear very favorably when compared with news commentator Milton Ouerbach of *B. F.'s Daughter*.

Probably the real point for Marquand was that he could never forget about the professional soldier's being both an officer *and* a gentleman. His Bob Tasmin of *B. F.'s Daughter* reflects upon the statement of Justice Oliver Wendell Holmes, who spoke of the Harvard graduates dead in the Civil War; to Tasmin they are "the few educated gentlemen who had made a gallant gesture that adorned the episode without in any way influencing the final results." Tasmin knew that such a statement would annoy Milton Ouerbach, who would have "gagged" at the word "gentleman" and who would have had considerable difficulty explaining the statement, coming as it did from the liberal justice of the Supreme Court.

Of the generals whom Tasmin met in his experience during the Pacific War, there were the men:

> Who were commanding the combat groups in a bloody, ruthless war, enigmatic men, whose final judgment was the same as destiny, though they would have simply said, if asked, that they were the first team out in the West Pacific carrying the ball. They were having their chance, at last, to justify their existence. No one had ever heard of them a year or two before, but now everyone was listening to them, searching for their human side and hanging on their jokes, which were not very good. They, too, would coin phrases which would appear in history—such things as "Damn the torpedoes!" "Fire when you are ready, Gridley," and "Don't give up the ship."

Or there were the new officers, the ninety-day wonders—like Polly's younger brother Harry—who, since they were not qualified by training or background, felt compelled to imitate the professional soldiers. Harry presented an imitation of General Mac-Arthur, all the mannerisms and the attitudes: "There was a similar outward thrust of the jaw, the same dauntless tilt of the head, the same half-careless and photogenic, but military, way of walking. If Harry had been carrying a cane or a swagger stick, he would have been a small model of MacArthur saying, 'I shall return.'"

I   Melville Goodwin, U.S.A.

By the time Marquand came to write *Melville Goodwin, U.S.A.*, however, he had decided to recognize officers and gentlemen as almost the last surviving anachronisms of our modern world. If no one else had any standards left, perhaps they might be found among the officers of the U.S. Army.

Looking back upon this novel a number of years after he had reviewed it unfavorably, Maxwell Geismar asks himself whether it was "really a plea for the provincial goodness of the Eisenhower-type personality in the modern age."[1] With this question Geismar suggests the difficulties which he, and no doubt many other readers, encountered in attempting to understand, or even explain, a phenomenon like General Melville Goodwin, U.S.A., who could emerge from a time of war, when he had proved himself possessed of a masterly professionalism, only to find himself victimized and very nearly destroyed during the peace which followed—destroyed by the excesses and the disorder, the absence of any personal discipline, and the general rejection of any set of values which might sustain the individual's integrity.

No doubt the character of Melville Goodwin was as unfamiliar to Marquand in the beginning as it was to some of his critics and his readers. But the instinct which led him to his attempt at interpretation was sound. The rule of the soldier, which Melville Goodwin apparently knew from boyhood, was that "action, correct or not, was preferable to immobility." And it was an axiom which had proved itself again and again in battle. The difficulty was that it didn't always seem applicable to civilian life, and in that case what did one do when confronted by decisions which called for resolution by the officer but which were always muddled through or entirely unresolved by the civilian?

Marquand seems to be suggesting that the individual out of uniform must be prepared for ready compromise, for moral ambiguity, for recognition of the relativity of values and judgments; but the soldier must, by the very nature of his profession, live by absolute standards of judgment, of value. He must act, and he must not question the decision which brings him to the action. The problem arises when the soldier must accomodate himself to the gradations of value which he inevitably discovers in civilian life.

The novel contrasts the attitudes toward experience of the narrator, Sidney Skelton, a radio commentator with a national reputation whose voice communicates a cultivated sense of integrity to his listeners, to those of Melville Goodwin whose own brand of integrity has made a courageous and assured commander of men in battle but which in the peace that follows bears a striking resemblance to ingenuousness and naïveté. Skelton has it made; and, though he frequently entertains the notion of rebellion, he probably understands that he will never revolt against a pattern of life for which he feels contempt even though it has brought him fame, a nation-wide audience, a beautiful wife, a luxurious home in the Connecticut countryside— and the knowledge that somewhere he missed a major turning, that he should have changed his route at the crossroads, that he should never have reached the point of no return.

Marquand writes as knowledgeably in *Melvin Goodwin* of the entertainment industry, of life behind the microphone and the editorial desks of the publishing industry, as he had written earlier of the foreign correspondent, the play-doctor, or the rising young banker. The pages devoted to a detailed exploration behind the scenes in broadcasting are as engrossing as any of Marquand's previous surveys of the kind; and the pretext which Marquand hits upon as a means of introducing the inevitable flash-backs seems entirely natural.

Melville Goodwin, a two-star general, stumbles onto the front pages of the nation's press when, quite by accident, he is responsible for intervening to avert a threatened clash between allied and Soviet patrols in Berlin. It was chance, too, that a press correspondent should have happened to be with him at the time. The resulting story made Melville Goodwin a hero over night—a hero, to be sure, in whose creation the Army was willing to assist if it might mean a score in the game of "upmanship" with the Air Force and the Navy. Because Sid Skelton had once met General Goodwin on a European front, he is commissioned to serve as his protector while the build-up of the hero is taking place in the United States. It was feared that the general could conceivably make a fool of himself and thus be responsible for destroying the image which was about to be projected for the public at home. Phil Bentley, correspondent for a Luce-style publication, has the assignment to interview the general and to write a full-length "profile" of a "hero in the making." In this way Marquand sets out to show through Melville Goodwin's reminiscences what it is that makes him the leader of men he is known to be.

The whole plan of the novel is extraordinarily interesting, and there certainly have been no more successful efforts to catch the significance of the professional soldier in his attempts to adjust to the demands of a peacetime world. Sid Skelton, remembering the officers of armies around the world whom he had met during his wartime travels, reflects that "it was always good-by to all that, for none of those people belonged in a peacetime setup, and it was the same with Melville Goodwin. He, too, was a throwback from the war, and he had already become a shadow. He was someone who would never be real again unless there was another war." Even so, there were things which Sid Skelton did not remember until later: that service friendships were less casual than those of the civilian world; that such friendships took the place of material accumulation and possession; that there was such a thing as service loyalty. He should have known, he confesses, "that Melville Goodwin was someone who would never say goodby."

II *Satiric Fiction*

I have written earlier, in reference to *H. M. Pulham, Esquire,* that the "straights" of the world—those who have not yet been deprived of their innocence, their faith, or their integrity—are not quite an extinct species. I have said that Marquand as a satirist was a very great lover first, that his satirical portraits were never etched in acid, and that his judgments always tended to be highly tentative. These points must be restated, for it has been assumed rather generally that we have seen an end to innocence, that the theme of innocence in the American novel as it was developed in the classic American novel of Cooper, Melville, and Mark Twain, must necessarily find expression today, if at all, in sentimentality or in the concept of violation of innocence—as in the novels of Carson McCullers. But Marquand never allowed himself to be persuaded that there was no longer a place for the "straights" of the world. And Marquand was never by intention a satirist in the tradition to which most of his critics have tended to assign him. Mr. Charles Brady has been unique among these critics because he has seen the manner in which most of them have misinterpreted the nature of Marquand's satire.

As an example, we refer to Nathan Cosman, who, writing in the *Nation* a few years back, asserted that "it would seem that achievement in satire goes rather to one who sticks to a choice in an issue than to one who changes his mind. To scorn and to embrace a subject alternately is not a virtue but an indulgence. It blurs distinctions, and, what is a worse crime, it destroys values. . . ."[2] Mr. Cosman is writing about Marquand's confessed fondness for George Apley, but his serious charge is without sympathy or understanding. Mr. Cosman is writing about one kind of satire; Marquand is creating another.

"He attacks but never to the limit," Mr. Cosman declares. We wonder why he should be expected to do so. After all, Marquand is not that kind of writer. As Professor Brady points out, "He has no ax to grind, political, economic, or otherwise. On this plane his fiction is neither philosophy nor journalism, but an imaginative and sympathetic series of insights into social man in our contemporary age of anxiety. From the standpoint of both capitalist and communist dialectic, he inevitably appears a pessimist even as, to the conventional bourgeois judgment of his day, Thackeray appeared a cynic. . . . Marquand neither indicts capitalist man or celebrates communist man. He merely judges acquisitive man and, if he indicts at all, indicts human nature."[3]

Marquand does not seek to destroy; loving his characters quite as much as he tends to regard them with an intelligently sharp objectivity, he cannot meet the requirements which Mr. Cosman demands of satire. His characters are too full-dimensioned for the kind of satirical treatment which Mr. Cosman mistakenly demands. Furthermore, Marquand is saying that in a world of such constantly shifting values it is quite impossible to stick, as Mr. Cosman demands, "to a choice in an issue." Marquand was much too intelligent either "to scorn or to embrace a subject alternatively," and his final treatment of his major characters is to see them as individuals and not as satirical caricatures.

III   *Values and Discipline*

Mr. Geismar, I suspect, labors under a similar misunderstanding, though his judgment is more readily defensible, even if more indicative of a contemporary willingless to reject a set of values attributed to the cultural background of the American small town of the early American twentieth century. While in Europe, Melville Goodwin falls in love with Dottie Peale, follows her from place to place, and after it is apparently all over, hears from her once more when he becomes a celebrity in the States. His career is endangered, his wife Muriel is made unhappy by her knowledge of her husband's compulsion, and his value as man and soldier is challenged. At the end he chooses to resume his life with the woman whose adult years have been shared with him. Yet Mr. Geismar asserts that "it might have taken more guts . . . if Melville Goodwin himself had really gone through with his disastrous affair with Dottie Peale."[4] We begin to wonder how far Mr. Geismar would have the fictional characters of the books he reviews carry his own emphasis on revolt.

In any case, *Melville Goodwin* is not concerned with revolt but with discipline, the kind which might provide peace, help for pain, or, at the very least, certitude. And there "on a darkling plain / Where ignorant armies clash by night" Mel Goodwin recalled the lines from "Dover Beach." "Perhaps he had learned at the Point that there was no peace nor help for pain, but he had been surrounded by certitude, even certitude of the hereafter."

The attitudes and values which young Mel Goodwin brought with him to West Point were those which the academy encouraged and which gave the greatest assurance of success. A small-town boy, he had been shaped by plain living and practical if not high thinking. As General Goodwin himself said, "it was a pretty good thing for a student at West Point to start as a pretty simple kid with just a few essential loyalties. It was a good thing for this hypothetical young lad to have been used to eating plain food, to sleeping in a cold room, to manual labor, and, above all, to telling the truth." West Point had made him what he was; never after the years there was he prepared to understand the "gold-bricking" of civilians taken into service, the "civilian gripes about the army and its discipline," and the eagerness of ninety-day wonders to put the army and all its works behind them as quickly as possible. He was, he knew, "in a different class with a different rating."

Muriel, too, was in a different class. She always understood the army, knew how to address one of Melville's superior officers from the beginning, knew how to say enough but not too much. Even in the year of their engagement and Melville's graduation from West Point, Muriel showed how well she knew the army when she expressed the hope that he would get an overseas assignment before the war in France came to an end back in 1918.

But Melville Goodwin, like so many of Marquand's characters before him, wondered if he had not missed something significant, something which might yield to him the last ultimate meaning. He asks Sid Skelton, "Sid, do you ever feel as though you'd missed something? I mean something you've never known about?" It is the age-old question. All of Marquand's characters can answer it in only one way: one can't have everything. Sid acknowledges that everyone has felt that way at some time, and certainly Sid has more than a little reason to know and understand Mel Goodwin's agitated inquiry. Mel Goodwin is strengthened by remembering "Old Ulysses" in Tennyson's poem. Says Goodwin to Sid Skelton, "Old Ulysses must have felt just that way, and he had the brains to recognize it." For Sid the simplicity of the inquiry is proof that people like Mel should not "mess around" with people like Sid—civilians, people who cannot or could not understand—for Sid says, "You can't be me, and I can't be you. Nobody can have everything." Nobody can have everything, and nobody can understand everybody. There is an inevitable barrier between soldiers and civilians, between discipline and the latitude of conduct and behavior which we associate with civilian life. But, of course, Goodwin belonged to an army generation which did not feel compelled to resign from duty in order to lecture the civilian population.

Mel Goodwin would like to share that quality of civilian life which he believes has been denied him. He wants to be a part of the irresponsibility, the sensual self-indulgence, the relativity of moral codes which characterizes our civilization —and yet, he knows that he can not really belong to this brave new postwar world of which he is supposed to be a part. Sid Skelton says that he wouldn't want to be Mel Goodwin; yet, understanding the rejection and the rudeness implied, he goes on to say that he couldn't be Mel Goodwin even if he tried. Sid knows that is the truth, for he could never approach Goodwin's degree of truth, honor, or integrity. For all the "sincerity" of his radio voice, Sid Skelton realizes that he is the "phony" and that Mel Goodwin is the uncomplicated but honorable figure of our time.

Marquand suggests that today all men wish to escape themselves, and Mel Goodwin is no exception. He doesn't wish to be himself, and he thinks that Dottie understands. Sid Skelton knows that Dottie doesn't want to be herself either, but for a reason that the general could never understand: Dottie doesn't know who she is and wouldn't know what she might become if the situation were to change for her. Dottie Peale doesn't know who she is at all, and Melville Goodwin *does* know himself; at least he had always known himself in the world of the military which had shaped him. And the officers in the Pentagon had known him. The point about Melville Goodwin was that he had always been so predictable, and dependable. Now that he had done something unexpected by having an affair, he was an unknown quantity. From the military standpoint it hardly seemed wise to proceed with the appointment of such an officer to Plans in the Pentagon. Other officers, of course, had been unfaithful to their wives; but, "when someone like Mel Goodwin suddenly took a stray," it was different: "It was hard to explain the difference, but it shook one's faith in institutions of regularity."

Sid Skelton was sure that the army would straighten out Goodwin's affairs; the army always took care of its own. And perhaps the solidity of Melville Goodwin, that quality of self-assured dependability, was responsible for the increasing admiration which Sid Skelton had come to feel for the general. He once reflected that "there was no solid Victorian future any longer. There were no William Ernest Henleys any longer, making us the masters of our fates and the captains of our souls." There is an irony in Sid's belief that he is indebted to General Goodwin for the new sense of security which he achieved after arriving in Chicago, over the head of his manager Gilbert Frary, to sew up the new contract for the continuing use of his "sincere" voice on radio and television. The irony lies in his conviction that Melville Goodwin has obtained his security without surrender of principle while he, Sid Skelton, is now only a piece of property who can never escape his fate because he is not the man Goodwin is; he doesn't have the "requisite self-belief." Yet at the end the general's wife Muriel makes it clear to Sid Skelton that she is not interested in saving their marriage simply for the love she feels, nor for personal possessiveness, but because the general is a valuable piece of army property which must not be destroyed by a foolish impulse and a neurotic woman.

The army *does* straighten out the general's troubled affairs; at least, Mel Goodwin's appointment to a command post in Japan before Korea and his avoidance of a desk job in Plans at the Pentagon straighten them out for him. Sid Skelton, who meets the general for the last time at the Waldorf in New York, spends the evening with him over a bottle of Scotch. Mel Goodwin had talked over the Dottie Peale episode with his wife Muriel just the night before, and she had agreed that the best and most honest thing would be for him to go to New York to straighten things out before they flew to Japan for their new assignment. The general, Sid discovers, is as happy as a school boy; Dottie took her rejection very well. Really, Sid should have seen her; she was truly a most remarkable woman. The general never had to know what Sid knew—that while he might not have everything, he had more than Dottie Peale would ever have, who had never begun to learn that "you had to give up some part of yourself to get anything you wanted." He knew, too, that "no man, nothing, would ever answer her desire," that the destructive force within which drove her would never permit her to achieve her desire. Sid knew that one Mel Goodwin was worth a thousand Dottie Peales, and that when he had been willing to give her everything, she was uninterested in anything he had to offer.

General Melville Goodwin was only "that God-damned brass-hat general of yours" to Dottie Peale; when the brass wore off, she asserted, there was only more brass underneath, and in those impossible civilian clothes of his it was just no use. "Disillusion," Sid Skelton understood, "always came from details." He knew, and the general didn't, of Dottie Peal's desperate confession: "Everything would have been possible if he'd only been a little more like other people, more like you and me, but he's so damned —so damned honest, darling." It was Sid who thought, when he heard her plea for help, that "you always had to pay for every party," and it was understandable that Dottie should have taken it so well when the general came to her with a confession that he had been a fool; for her the payment had been deferred once more.

So, finally, what kind of man was this Major General Melville Goodwin, whose wife Muriel was so ambitious for him and wished to see him add another star to those he already wore? The reader may see him through the eyes of Muriel Goodwin who spent an evening with the Skeltons recounting the events of the general's career. Those events had become as vivid to Sid Skelton as "the footage of a documentary film."

There was little Mel Goodwin fighting that Stickney boy at school, Mel Goodwin studying algebra with Muriel Reece, the first kiss at the Sunday school picnic, Goodwin at the Point, and Goodwin, captain of Company A. I was with him near Chateau-Thierry when the machine guns opened up. I encountered him walking back wounded in North Africa, and I could hear the enlisted man saying that he was a God-damned fighting bastard, those words that he wanted on his tombstone. Melville Goodwin had been an officer who earned every cent of money that the taxpayers had paid out on him.

There is, then, *that* General Goodwin; there is, further, the General Goodwin whose career and whose character have so obviously intrigued Marquand the novelist. *This* general is somewhat more ambiguous, a combination of the simple and the shrewd, who is seen through the eyes of disillusioned narrator Sid Skelton. And finally there is the general seen by a largely unsympathetic reviewer like Maxwell Geismar; and this character is the symbol of all that Mr. Geismar disapproves of in Marquand's later work:

The whole point about Melville Goodwin as an army officer is that his code of behavior is honest. He believes in his career completely and puts it to the test in the field of combat. A good man if kept in his place; but is this the only possible solution for the problem of belief in a commercial society without established forms of tradition? It might have taken more guts, a word which Marquand's General approves of, if Sid had really abandoned his voice and put his mind to work, or if Melville Goodwin himself had really gone through with his disastrous affair with Dottie Peale. But in the struggle with "authority" that runs through Marquand's work, authority, even if stale or false, always wins. The soldier's code is a logical refuge for his disgruntled bankers and despairing playwrights.[5]

Mr. Geismar has a point, but he makes rather too much of it. Marquand, it is obvious, was attracted to the character of Mel Goodwin precisely because he has a code, shared by Muriel Goodwin, by which his conduct and his life are shaped; namely, as defined by Muriel Goodwin, that "the service is more important than Mel or me." Mr. Geismar has a point insofar as he is quite correct in assuming that there must be some authority, some standard of values, some code of conduct for the characters of a social novelist, a novelist of manners, unless he is finally to surrender the concept that any cultural pattern, any accepted standards and values of an on-going civilization are within the realm of the possible. Is the authority of Melville Goodwin really as "false and stale" as Mr. Geismar says? Certainly Marquand must have felt otherwise; or, if he had finally come to concur, it must have been the worse for him as a novelist.

It must be said that Marquand never did surrender the possibility of there being some value to be saved from the spiritual shipwreck of our times. He never abandoned the Arnoldian and Christian conviction that when a few persons are gathered together there may be a community which can speak to and understand one another. He knew always, as Dottie Peale never did know, that "you had to give up some part of yourself to get anything you wanted." That is a very different thing from Mr. Geismar's assumption that Sid Skelton had to obey the general's final directive out of a sense of allegiance to authority and to make good in the radio profession "for the sake of his wife and kiddies." The charge not only misses Marquand's point entirely but also is more than a little unfair. Marquand's understanding of contemporary American life seems more profound that Geismar's. We can hardly sympathize with Mr. Geismar's implied rewriting of Marquand with happy revolutionary endings which lead all the organization men to throw over the security they had struggled to gain for assistant professorships in fourth-rate colleges across the land.

There had been times during Melville Goodwin's trial and testing when Sid Skelton could wish that he might be back in the "ETO again, in a world without women," and he wished on those occasions that Melville Goodwin might have died, "as he very well might have and should have, in North Africa or Salerno or somewhere along the Rhine." Remembering the life that Melville Goodwin had lived, and the meaning of it, Sid Skelton had the courage to tell his wife that there were times when "men like to lead lives of their own . . . , or they like to be allowed to think they do. Now take me. I don't always like what's arranged for me either—but I haven't Goodwin's guts."

Sid did not admire the officers in the Pentagon, career men who had combat training and experience, without realizing their limitations, for "war always gave those people too much power. Its fumes still remained in their heads like old Burgundy from the night before. Even the best of them developed a Messiah complex, once they had the rank. If they gave the word, they still expected you to snap into it with pleasure, always secure in the belief that their own affairs were of paramount significance." Sid Skelton could understand and see the limitations of the military mind in times of peace, but yet he could not cancel out the significance of the contribution that the Melville Goodwins were able to make to America at peace or at war.

On that last evening together with Sid Skelton, General Goodwin let it be known with no evasion that he expected to get through on Sid's private phone without silly civilian delays. "'When I try to get you on the telephone, son,' he said, 'I want to get through to you without telling my life history. Get this arranged in the future when I call you, will you?'" And Sid promised, despite himself, that he would. General Goodwin assumed that he had made a friend, that Sidney Skelton had been through so much with him there was no longer any question of his right to pull rank upon him or to have rank pulled, even from a civilian. And probably Sid Skelton felt the same way. The journalist could even put up with the general's favorite quotation from Tennyson which he recited on every conceivable occasion: "Push off and sitting well in order smite." Perhaps the general had made a friend. So far as Skelton was concerned, the explanation of Mel's conduct was his corny morality, the simplicity of his pattern of life.

It was, Sid concluded, this essential innocence which saved Goodwin in the Dottie Peale affair: "The clear truth of his innocence explained his aberration." If Goodwin didn't understand women, neither did women (in the person of Dottie Peale) understand him (though Muriel Goodwin did and managed to make the most of his ignorance). At the same time Sid Skelton knew that Mel Goodwin would always be an "Old Glory" boy. He knew the type, even though it was one he could not possibly emulate. Mel Goodwin was just more honest than most people, or so Marquand tells us. And Marquand seems willing to leave it at that:

> For some reason or other, nothing in that confession [Mel's to Sid] sounded tawdry or shopworn, when every element in it should have. Something in Melville Goodwin prevented it. There was always a quality in him of simple fact that raised him above the obvious. There was a metal that life had never tarnished, though it possessed a confusing luster for people like Dottie Peale and me. He was a stranger from a strange world which we could never touch.

"We've been through a hell of a lot together." Those are almost the last words of Mel Goodwin to Sid Skelton, representatives of two worlds. But they know they are not likely to meet again. And who has the better of the meeting? It doesn't seem likely that Marquand is primarily sympathetic with his struggling enterpriser, but then neither is it apparent that authority, "stale or false" or any other kind, has become the "logical refuge for [Marquand's] disgruntled bankers and despairing playwrights." That Melville Goodwin has a "code" is clear enough; he summarizes it rather simply as he explains his reasons for ending the affair with Dottie Peale. To do so, he states, did not take guts: "It's only truth. There are some things you have to lay on the line—some things. For instance . . . ," there was the flag and the men he led whom he could not ask to do things he would not do himself, and none of that had anything to do with "guts," he insisted. It was nothing more than an uncomplicated expression of a need for personal integrity, of belief in principle.

Such a code, so simply expressed and so faithfully held, could hardly have served as any kind of refuge for the cynical or disillusioned intellectual in the democracy of twentieth-century America, nor did Marquand intend it to be understood as such.

We shall be closer to the truth when we understand that while democracy in our time must be "multanimous" (to borrow a word for universal acceptance coined by Crane Brinton) it need not at the same time reject the possibility of faith, or tradition, or belief; it very definitely does *not* mean—and this, I believe, comes closer to expressing Marquand's own conviction—that, in Brinton's words, "no one should *really* believe in God, or the life-force, or Science (with a capital S), or the Single Tax, it does not mean that in a democracy men should all be cynics, skeptics, or at least Laodiceans." What it does mean, on the contrary, Mr. Brinton points out, is that, though one need not love, one must not kill, or imprison, or close the gathering places of the unconverted—and the unconvertible; that one must "at least pay them sincerely the kind of respect he pays to the weather, or his wife, or anything else he knows he can't change."[6]

As a summary of John Marquand's social thought in the year 1951, perhaps no better statement could be offered. Sid Skelton and General Melville Goodwin belong to different worlds which nevertheless were capable of touching, understanding in a degree, and tolerating one another. That this is so, indicates a continuing strength of the social order they share—as well as a measure of the sympathetic understanding possessed by Marquand as artist in his depiction of that order.

CHAPTER 8

"Look forward, not back"

IN *Sincerely, Willis Wayde* (1955) Marquand turned his attention to the organization man at a time when the "business novel" and a series of sociological studies were receiving widespread public acceptance. In this novel Marquand is once more, as even Maxwell Geismar rather grudgingly owns, the "acute and often brilliant observer of middle-class manners," and one possessed of the "merciless eye of a born reporter, the sensitive ear for speech, the gift of creating atmosphere and social types." His protagonist rises from the ranks, not of labor but of the white-collar class, to become the organization man's organization man; or, as Geismar trenchantly puts it, "the lonely boss of the lonely crowd."[1]

Without ranking it comparatively, *Sincerely, Willis Wayde* certainly deserves an honorable place among the great novels of American business, from Howells' *Silas Lapham* through Dreiser's *The Titan* and *The Financier* and Sinclair Lewis' *Dodsworth*. But Willis Wayde is no individualist like those protagonists of the earlier business novel; he represents a later social type created by the big corporations, scientific business methods, and the "managerial revolution." Indeed, as a character he stands in marked contrast to the independent Wayde, Sr., who will sell his services but not his soul. As a barometer of the cultural and social trends of the times, Marquand is as brilliantly effective as he has ever been.

I *Basic Themes and Conflicts*

Once more, too, we have a familiar conflict between "new" money and "old" money, represented respectively by the ambitious Willis Wayde and "by the aristocratic Harcourts of New England." The aspirations of the "lower-upper" class hero for acceptance by the "upper-upper" class Harcourts—and in particular by Henry Harcourt's granddaughter Bess—repeat the social theme of *Point of No Return*. And once again there is the theme of "so little time." Willis Wayde doesn't have time for the activities that most young men engage in, for girls and for social life, since the drive for business success is so compelling. When his father understands the direction of his son's course, he expresses regret that he ever brought him from Arizona to New England and the Harcourt mills, and urges him to find time for living as an average normal boy is supposed to live. But Willis reminds his father that he went through college in three years (Boston University, not Harvard where Mr. Harcourt had offered to send him) and that he has been working summers: "I understand what you mean, partly, but I don't have much time."

Father Wayde serves to introduce yet another theme, the development and illustration of which occupy most of the remaining pages of the book. Alfred Wayde, a skilled machinist who has been given every inducement by the Harcourts to stay on with the mills as an almost indispensable consultant, values his independence so much that he could never be something which he isn't, and that, he fears, is precisely what his son is attempting to do. He tells Willis: "You keep on trying to be something you aren't and you'll end up a son of a bitch. You can't help being, if you live off other people." His father, Willis recognized, was describing the gap which exists between the creator and the entrepreneur who use the creator's gifts for his own ends:

> "Listen, boy," he said. "People are divided into two parts— people who do things and the rest, who live off those who do things. Now I may not amount to much, but I've had a pretty happy time, because I can turn out something. I can do anything in that damn mill that anyone else can do, and they all know it, boy. Well, maybe you'll spend your life living off other people's doings, but if you have to, don't fool yourself. Maybe you'll end up like Harcourt. I don't know. But you'll never be like Harcourt."

Willis would never be like Harcourt, finally, because there were no more Harcourts; the Willis Waydes and what they represented had destroyed them. The "good" capitalists with their paternalistic concerns and their company towns—like the Harcourt's Mill Town at the edge of Clyde—had given way;

they were crowded out of the picture by the great accumulations of capital with their corporate structures.

No doubt Father Wayde was right about the probable end of his son if he persisted in attempting to be something he was not. Young Willis, for all of his rough edges, was a likeable young man; but after the polish was applied it was difficult to know precisely what Willis Wayde really was. At the end, when Willis and his wife are taking the vacation in Paris which they had promised themselves for so long, he meets a former acquaintance from Clyde quite by chance at a sidewalk café. Just recently Willis had found himself forced to close the Harcourt mill which had come to be, as he saw it, a losing proposition. Though it was almost like cutting off his arm, as he said, he simply had to do it. The acquaintance couldn't say whether the sincere expressions of regret were really sincere at all. He was now a different Willis Wayde from the one whom Clyde had known years before. The former acquaintance reflected that "it might very well have been that he did have a soft spot in his heart, and that he had honestly meant what he said about loyalty, and about being deeply sorry. On the other hand he might have had no heart at all. Authority and success had made him strangely impervious, since success had smoothed down all his rough edges, turning him into a type interchangeable with any photograph on the financial page of the *New York Times*. It was hard to tell about those people, who had all been processed in the same way, but he was essentially an American type."

The memorable climax comes immediately after, with coincidence being screwed just a bit tighter as the Willis Waydes meet Bess Harcourt and her husband at the same café, a meeting which is unavoidable. Sincerely, Willis extends his hand with a cheery greeting; the hand is ignored and so is the greeting. "'You're in my way, Willis,' she said. 'Get out.'" And when he protests amiably, and sincerely, "'You're in my way,' Bess repeated and then she laughed in that bright malicious way of hers. 'Get out, Uriah Heep.'" But as Willis walked away, Steve Decker, a former acquaintance from Clyde, reflected that one couldn't help admiring Willis Wayde. He had come a long way since he had lived at the Harcourt place.

After that encounter at the café it didn't very much matter for a time what he had become—not even after his wife Sylvia had soothed him and reassured him and given him his Nembutal; for he was right back once more to the time when he had been the "boy" living in the cottage on the Harcourt estate, and Bess Harcourt could tell him that she didn't mind at all going places with him—". . . . when there isn't anyone else around." Or when she announced that she had to kiss a boy sometime "and I may as well get it over with. Go ahead." Or when, a few years later, home for vacation from Boston University, he was invited once more to kiss her in the woods, and it was different. However, she said that it was all right so long as it was only here; but she didn't know why she was such a fool. " 'You see we both belong in other places,' she said, 'and we can't help that, can we?' " And Willis thought that perhaps that was the wisest thing she had ever said to him, and that probably she really had more common sense than he. He didn't remember the words of his father on this occasion, but well he might have.

There at the café, while speaking with his former acquaintance, Willis Wayde had a good deal to say about loyalty. Indeed, the word falls frequently from his tongue, as do "sincerity" and "basically." Willis Wayde is "basically" a sincere and loyal person. The interesting thing about the novel is the way in which Marquand reveals, gradually and subtly, the development of a style and a manner in Willis Wayde. Words representing values become in the course of the novel little more than useful tools employed in the art and science of self-projection. Before his marriage to Sylvia, daughter of a Harvard professor and a thoroughly inexplicable mate for a Willis Wayde, he explains his reasons for leaving one firm to join another which will advance his career. She asks if such a move would not be disloyal since his employers had sent him to the firm which he now proposes to join. Loyalty had nothing whatsoever to do with the situation, he tried to explain. But women could never understand. He was making his way, making a place for himself, and that hadn't anything to do with loyalty. "Loyalty," he reflected, "was the damnedest thing. It was something that kept cropping up in business at eccentric intervals, and it kept requiring a different definition. . . . You had to do the best you could with loyalty." Perhaps his confusion was entirely understandable, for he had learned that the car one drove and the golf score one could show were significant criteria of measurement in the business world. These standards violated the rules his father had laid down, but he still found it necessary to give up his Ford runabout for a new Buick. Sylvia said, when she saw it, that she hoped people wouldn't think they were throwing their weight around; but Willis said never mind, just "wait until we get our Cadillac before you start to worry."

If the marriage with Sylvia Hodges seems inexplicable, the reason must be principally that at this period Willis Wayde was attempting to smooth off the rough edges in earnest; Sylvia is in despair because he can talk only about the Buick and because he forgets that the groom must buy the bridal bouquet, must select a ring, and certainly should express a desire to see the wedding gifts. But Willis is learning to cover all his omissions and his inadvertencies by resorting to a feigned innocence and an excessive uxoriousness. His remarks addressed to Sylvia are liberally sprinkled with "sweetness," and "darlings," and "dears." It is a characteristic of Willis' relationship with his wife which finds increasing emphasis as his dependence upon her grows. And the reader becomes aware that Willis Wayde, despite his success in the terms by which his world measures success, is one of those American males who will prolong adolescence until middle age. He is like Hemingway's Francis Macomber who never finds, however, a real testing of his own manhood in the course of the novel.

Alfred Wayde, the father, provides a further uneasy note of warning when he and Willis' mother come to Cambridge for the wedding. He had permitted his son and his wife to talk him into wearing one of those "monkey suits," but he has his reservations about the course which Willis has chosen.

"Now, son," he said, and his voice was warm and gentle. "I know you've got to get along like all the rest of us. Boys like you have to try to be something they're not in order to get ahead, and if you try hard enough, no doubt you'll be what you want to be. You're marrying a real nice girl. She's a little thin for my taste, but no doubt she'll flesh out. There's only one thing that bothers me."

He stopped and lighted his pipe again.

"Just don't get too smooth," he said, "or you'll turn into a son of a bitch. A lot of people do before they know it, son."

Willis recalled that he had received similar counsel from his father on a previous occasion. But perhaps he never fully realized just how smooth he was getting to be. He had never been one to make friends; the loyalty of friendship never had occasion to be brought to the test. From childhood he had been an outsider. One point of the novel appears to be that, as his power in the world of industry increases, his concepts of "loyalty" and "friendship" become increasingly tainted by monetary considerations. It was difficult to be trusting, to be "friends forever" as Bess Harcourt hoped they might be, when he suspected that her sincerity might have been prompted by an ulterior motive, as she perhaps suspected his might be. When Willis has become powerful enough to gain virtual control of Harcourt Mills through his stock purchases, and he and Sylvia are invited to the Harcourt home for a social evening before the stockholders' meeting on the following day, Sylvia comments upon how deeply fond of him the Harcourts obviously are—and how implicity they trust him. Willis feels and asserts that she is exaggerating; they don't trust him as much as all that. When Sylvia assures him that they do indeed, that they have expressed the fullest confidence in him, Willis reflects that "it was hard to explain why instead of being warmed by Sylvia's remark, it aroused a hostile and resentful feeling. The Harcourts, of course, had to depend on someone because of their utter incapacity, and he was surpised that Sylvia did not appear to recognize the fact." This reflection is a disquieting preparation for almost inevitable betrayal of trust.

He is ready to take advantage of the Harcourts' trust and incompetence if possible, though he is not ready to admit it, even to himself. He only wished that Bess Harcourt hadn't been quite so friendly with Sylvia, quite so kind; and he wished that the Harcourts weren't all trust and dependence. Willis, even at that stage, was capable of recognizing sophistry; but so long as there was a grain of truth, he clung to the grain, no matter how diminutive. Willis Wayde had become a master of words, and as time passed it became less and less difficult for him to be carried away by his own rhetorical sophistries, even as he belittled his own words. He assures Mr. Bryson Harcourt that he is there only to help him, to take routine details off his hands; yet even while he is urging him, the son of his benefactor, to "put him in his place" if he gets out of line, he is preparing to manipulate and control Harcourt Mills. He is also preparing to receive Bess Harcourt's final contemptuous dismissal of him as "Uriah Heep." And, without blanching, Willis Wayde can hear Mr. Harcourt speak the words as president which Willis had insinuated into his mind: "All he [Willis] wants, he told me, is to have our enterprise succeed, and then he added that he would always stand loyally behind me. Knowing him, I have learned to accept his loyalty and integrity as axiomatic. It is with more reluctance that I accept his modesty. I ask you for a rising toast to our new vice-president, Mr. Willis Wayde." Willis Wayde, who tried never to lose a good effect, recalled the importance of that principle when, following his brief and calculatedly moving response to the tribute, he hesitated momentarily before resuming his seat. The applause demonstrated that he had his timing right.

Marquand's character has learned all of the requisite gestures and factitious mannerisms which qualify him for winning friends and influencing people. He always strives for the calculated effect, even when he is most "sincere." Bess Harcourt seems to challenge his sincerity after she has heard his response on that occasion. When he tells her that he meant every word he said and assures her that "what's more, I'm in the habit of meaning what I say," he really believes it—and, almost, he makes Bess Harcourt believe it. The fact is that Willis Wayde *does* believe; but, more important, he does not realize that he no longer understands the meaning of any value. He has reached the relativistic point of no return in the corporate world, a never-never land where any values are concerned.

II *Conditioned Men*

Marquand wrote *Willis Wayde* prior to the Justice Department's prosecution of the electric companies' officialdom, but Willis was of their company. Marquand makes his point clearly enough, if we desire to see it. Willis was a home-loving, church-going, civic-institution-supporting, 100-per cent American who was worth more, as more than one "desk jockey" at the Pentagon assured him, than at least a couple of companies of infantry and an air squadron, even though he never got into uniform. His companies won more than their share of "E" flags and commendations by Army, Navy, and Air Force. And yet, as a man, he violated something in himself, assisted others to violate their essential integrity—and all in the name of integrity—with a capital *I*. It was essential to win the war, of course, and Marquand was as conscious of the necessity as anyone else, as his overage enlistment, his Intelligence service in Washington and in the Far East could testify. But during and after the war, he must have seen a lot of Willis Waydes. The criticism so often made of Marquand's work—that he did not take a firm stand regarding the objects of his satirical consideration, that he temporized—this criticism is understandable. Yet, Marquand was an honest novelist, and it is hard to conceive of a talented writer living in our time—particularly one so acutely aware of the latest social and cultural trends as was Marquand—who would not recognize moral ambiguity of the life of a corporate magnate who could enter into a conspiracy to fix monopolistic prices at the same time that he was acting as superintendent of the Sunday school in his own particular exurbanite community.

In short, Marquand's point is that Willis Wayde is not really the son of a bitch his father has suspected him of being. In the eyes of his generation he is not even a Uriah Heep—if the term could possibly mean anything to his contemporaries. He is one of Marquand's conditioned men of the modern world. He is a man who will, to the end of his days, continue to sign himself, "Sincerely, Willis Wayde"; what is more, Willis will mean every word of it.

Critics have objected that *Willis Wayde* seems not to resolve any issues; and it has been asserted that the moral conflicts of Willis Wayde are never made quite clear. But this contention seems rather to miss the point: nothing in this world is ever quite clear to Willis Wayde. Indeed, the significant point is that nothing can ever be quite clear in the milieu of which Willis Wayde is a part. One does not dominate this world which men like Willis Wayde know; on the contrary, such men are dominated by it. He is the sort of character who can reflect his era by buying a mansion and grounds which he cannot afford, and who can reply to his wife's protests with, "if there's any ostentation, we'll outgrow it mighty quickly." In a world which allows one to outgrow ostentation, Marquand implies, what values can one cling to which have any right to be seriously considered as binding beyond the next purchase of a larger and a gaudier residence? Or, as Willis Wayde himself said when he sold the ostentatious mansion, "In life and in business, you couldn't stand still in America." In Willis Wayde's world, what was a home for if not primarily to have a legitimate, tax-free place to offer entertainment to one's business associates? Sylvia, his wife, may say at this point, "I never thought you could be so fantastic, Willis," but the reader is hardly surprised. Willis

Wayde finally sells his mansion for a convalescent home—after dividing the property into lots—but there can be no home where Willis may convalesce. When the Harcourt mill is finally closed and the shock of the economic disaster is fully felt in the town of Clyde, Willis Wayde still receives the benefit of the doubt, despite the many bitter words expressed by those who suffer most from the disruption of the town's economic life. Clyde continued its unswerving loyalty toward one of its own and found it impossible to question the Integrity and Sincerity of Willis Wayde. Not even "treachery and disaster—such was the loyalty of Clyde—could . . . destroy the myth of Willis Wayde. There were those who even believed he would return in his Cadillac some day and repurchase and run the Harcourt Mill again."

The letter he wrote to Bess Harcourt at the time—which, to be sure, was never answered—provides the most revealing portrait of the later Willis Wayde, that boyish, middle-aged industrial tycoon who had finally made his fifteen minutes a day with the Harvard Classics pay off in the end:

> But, Bess, dear, let us not repine, but instead keep the memory of the Old Mill green in our sentiments. Agonizing though this whole decision is, I know that you and Bill, who now hold substantial blocks of Simcoe stock, will in the end come to my way of thinking. In the final analysis, deeply though our affections may be rooted in the past, you and I and all of the rest of us who have homes and families to care for, must look down the road ahead. As a fine, old New England preacher (was it Ralph Waldo Emerson?) once succinctly put it: "Look up, not down. Look forward, not back, and lend a hand."

III *A Question of Innocence*

It is doubtful if Willis Wayde ever quite understood what had happened to him, or whether he perceived in the slightest degree the part he had played in the betrayal of those values of an older order which died with the death of all the Clydes throughout the nation. He always assumed that he simply took the older way of life, re-created and streamlined it for greater efficiency, and had as a result a slicker and more functional design; that was as true of his business methods and ethics as it was of the mansions he built for his family, like that one in Lake Forest after he had moved to Chicago as vice-president to the far-flung Simcoe Corporation. Such a mansion was really more of an investment than a luxury, as he reminded a curious visitor from Clyde who had dropped by on the off-chance that he might be able to sell Willis Wayde some insurance. This home, as the visitor was quick to point out, obviously had incorporated many of the feature of the old Harcourt mansion back in Clyde, even down to the rhododendrons bordering the drive and the artificial pond with a swan on it; the tennis court too, Willis confessed, had been constructed from his memories of the one which Bess and Bill Harcourt had played upon so many years before. But, of course, in all-important particulars the place was extremely modern, with picture windows and all that—a kind of streamlined plant for living.

An interesting essay might be written on the nature of American innocence during the seventy years which separate *The Rise of Silas Lapham* and *Sincerely, Willis Wayde*. I have spoken of Willis Wayde's "feigned innocence," which, like the mask of legend, finally becomes indistinguishable from the face which has worn it for so long. Silas Lapham's "innocence" results in the eventual growth of self-knowledge and understanding so that, in the face of adversity resulting from financial reversal and ruin, his fall can be said to mark his real rise: his achievement of moral stature and a truer measure of success. With Willis Wayde the opposite is true. As he achieves his fantastic success in the terms by which the world measures success, he deliberately, though unwittingly, blinds himself to any fine discriminations of value; he lives by platitude and conveniently assembled copy-book maxims. He increasingly rationalizes his motives for conduct by sentimental self-justification and with cloying uxoriousness. His picture of the past is a creation of his own making which serves to justify his uncritical acceptance of his present self. He likes to think that he will be sending his children to a private school just outside Concord because, as he tells his Clyde visitor, "Sylvia and I have put our heads together to see what we can do to give our children the benefits of that New England heritage that you and I both value." He has become, without ever quite knowing it and certainly without acknowledging any possibility of it to himself, pretty much what his father had predicted he would become if he got "too smooth," too polished at the edges. And just as certainly, while he may have ended up like Harcourt, he never could be like Harcourt—as his father had pointed out so long before.

IV *Assessment of Willis Wade*

Notwithstanding the many virtues of *Sincerely, Willis Wayde* as a novel and as a perceptive and revealing study of the organization man of the modern business community, the reader probably will find it the least satisfactory of Marquand's major efforts. The character of Willis Wayde may be credible enough, even though he obviously never is capable of achieving self-knowledge or the realization that in gaining the whole world he may very probably have lost his soul. But despite his credibility, it is difficult to feel any real concern for him as an individual. He is incapable of the examined life; and in the presentation of his past, in once more resorting to the technique of flash-back as he has in previous novels, Marquand provides us with no pretext for doing so. Willis Wayde is no Harry Pulham, no Charles Grey, not even a Jeffrey Wilson. Willis Wayde uses the past, if at all, not as a means of revealing and giving meaning to, but of obscuring and distorting the significance of the present.

Marquand depends largely in this novel upon his favorite device of ironic presentation, and the revelation, when it comes, is revelation only to the reader and not to the protagonist. Willis Wayde follows the advice which he gave Bess Harcourt in his egregious letter: "Look forward, not back." And he might well have added, "Look outward, not inward." For there is no "inwardness," no self-examination possible to Willis Wayde. He is probably the only one of Marquand's major creations about whom we can feel at the end an almost complete indifference, unless, indeed, the feeling which prevails is a mild contempt. In one other novel, *The Late George Apley,* we may, to be sure, feel what might be termed a mildly amused contempt, but there it is directed largely toward the fictitious narrator, pedantic Mr. Horace Willing; George Apley himself, despite the screen of pedantry between him and the reader, emerges pretty well, and we are never unaware of the quality of sympathy and compassion which marks the novelist's own attitude toward his character. Neither can we miss Apley's own recognition, of which Willing of course is unaware, that the examined life has revealed the spiritually crippling limitations with which birth and conditioning have hedged him round.

Following Marquand's death Edward Weeks, writing in *The Atlantic Monthly,* reported a conversation with the novelist regarding the character of Willis Wayde which is even harsher than our discussion of him. Mr. Weeks remarked that while Wayde "had started out as a rather appealing young man," he wound up as "a truly disgusting individual." " 'That is certainly right,' John replied, as if surprised himself by Wayde's excesses. 'He turned out to be a real stinker, didn't he?' "[2] It is certainly a conclusion with which most readers would find it easy enough to agree.

What seem unsatisfactory features of the novel really indicate a far more serious failure which lies probably not in the book itself but in the materials composing the novel; these weaknesses are, in short, due to what Marquand apparently felt to be, and what a recent critic has termed, "the American Failure." The nature of that "failure" and its influence upon Marquand as a historian in fiction of manners and morals in mid-century America can perhaps be more fully explored in a detailed examination of Marquand's final novel, *Women and Thomas Harrow*. For unlike his Willis Wayde, a character for whom Marquand obviously felt little sympathy or compassion despite the fascination Wayde held for him as a uniquely significant social phenomenon, Marquand could look only backward, not forward, in his efforts to give the present meaning. His last novel essays once more the appraisal of our time in terms of a generation's experience. Having considered his final restatement of the recurring questions and his last tentative answers, we may then attempt an evaluation of the achievements and the limitations of John P. Marquand, novelist.

CHAPTER 9

The Defeat of the Past

I *The Social Novelist in America*

MARQUAND'S 1957 contribution is a slight, two-finger exercise entitled *Life at Happy Knoll* in which the reader is presented with the minor misadventures of the country-club set. Certainly the modern country-club is an interesting enough, perhaps even a significant, phenomenon of the American social scene; and Marquand may even have enjoyed writing about the members of Happy Knoll more than any other group of characters that he had previously presented, as he asserted was the case. But nonetheless the material is very thin and the characters which emerge from his straight epistolary method are little more than shadows. P. G. Wodehouse did this type of fiction much better.

The separate episodes gathered together to make the book had originally appeared in *Sports Illustrated* where they were very well received, but Marquand found it impossible to discover a really significant subject in his material. His principal character, President Emeritus Albert Magill of the Happy Knoll Country Club, who was constantly being asked for financial contributions, expresses a final disillusioned rejection of country-club values which we may suspect was shared by Marquand. He writes: "I fully realize, and believe you do too, that the Happy Knoll Country Club is not in itself an institution of profound importance, but only a superficial manifestation of bourgeois culture. Happy Knoll and other places like it appear in the end only rather crude efforts to escape from a few of the more unpleasant realities that surround us. Why else should one play golf?" But, of course, Marquand's own attitude toward this "manifestation of bourgeois culture" was as ambivalent as it was toward other aspects of the time. He could enjoy wearing the "canary-yellow-and-red tie" of the country club just as he could enjoy writing humorously about it. And he could turn with a continuing ambivalence of feeling to the more serious subject of the defeat of the past in the novel which followed his report on the American country club, even though we feel he must have recognized the nature of Thomas Harrow's almost inevitable failure before he put the first word on paper.

Alfred Kazin concludes his excellent review of *Women and Thomas Harrow* (1958), with this statement: "The social novelist in America pays for his lack of ideas when he is left without the social traditions on which he has depended so long for his sustenance as a man and his achievement as an artist."[1] These are disturbing words, for they suggest what may be an accurate estimate of Marquand's dilemma as an artist in his last years, and we wish it were not so. If we know Marquand's work really well and have followed its development from beginning to end, we feel an almost personal regret that there should have been a kind of betrayal involved—a betrayal which it is impossible to attribute to any human agency but is rather a result of the social and technological forces which have transformed modern America into something rare and strange—into a nation which no longer clings to, or even remembers, traditions or the values or the relationships of peoples which permitted continuity of standards within the republic.

The social novelist in America—a Marquand, an O'Hara, a Cozzens—has been convinced of the vulgarization of the American faith, and he has found it increasingly difficult to base his evaluations of our culture upon any fundamental principle. As Mr. Kazin points out, we have seen just how angry and disgusted Mr. James Gould Cozzens could become about the fact of the degradation of the republic in *By Love Possessed*, "whose essential tone is unlimited and profane bitterness. . . ."[2] More recently, we might have observed how far some leaders of the republic have strayed from the basic concept of the American Constitution as an (imperfect) reflection of the Divine and the Platonic laws, changeless and eternal, of the moral law which, according to Emerson, lies at the center of nature and radiates to its circumference, and of America as the "last best hope of earth." The social novelist in our time has sought to preserve the concept of law, of order, of traditional value in the midst of accelerated change and flux. He has provided documentation of the conclusion recently drawn by John Gunther in a popular magazine article: ". . . with the future of the nation, Western society and civilization itself at stake, no less, we still have room in our daily lives for . . . much that is indulgent, bigoted, irresponsible and, perhaps worst of all, frivolous."[3]

Mr. Gunther the journalist asks the American people the question which Marquand the novelist had been occupied with for at least twenty years.

> Today, the issue must be squarely faced: *Are* we a serious country? Do we really appreciate deeply enough, strongly enough, the stunning, irreversible changes that have come to the world in the past quarter century? Do we really understand that the world we accepted so complacently 25 years ago is gone forever and that life can never, never, never be the same again? And do we truly comprehend the basic grim character of the challenges that have arisen?[4]

Marquand's answers, implicit in his novels, are grimly but honestly negative; they are the basis for his increasing despair. To assert, as one American political voice has recently done, that "the rule of law is nonsensical and a waste of time. . . ."[5], may be legitimate as opinion but is dangerous as principle. Actually the "rule of law" stands foremost as an American principle; for only law, the reflection of some value not subject to change or caprice, is capable of supporting the very foundations of the republic— and the point was as well understood by Whitman as by Jefferson, good sons of the Enlightenment that they were.

To repudiate the article of faith now is to remove the very foundation of the society which, as Mr. Kazin asserts, has never really wanted to be a society. It is a society, he declares, ". . . in which individuals distrust the very idea of society, in which social distinctions are considered immoral or irrelevant as they are solitary voyagers like Ishmael, to whom the world is a metaphysical problem. Since the social novelist, by the very nature and accessibility of his material, is likely to be prolific and fluent, he must not exploit the fluency of his manner to describe a purely personal crisis. We want to see the relationships of people who are divided by class; we want to see human beings rise above class but not be unconvincingly free of class."[6] We are touched, he points out, by George Apley's being compelled to give up his Irish girl, for we recognize the need of the individual to defy convention even as we are aware of the binding force of convention itself. But after *Apley*, Kazin believes, Marquand faced increasing difficulties as a social novelist; in part because as his characters are drawn from a later generation, Marquand's own generation, it becomes evident that the protagonists are themselves too deeply involved in the spiritual malaise of the period to maintain the proper perspective toward it, and that the outlines of the conventions which Apley took for granted have become increasingly vague and shadowy. The result is that, having no longer a stable tradition as a criterion for evaluation of the present, the social novelist now "finds himself crying out against the absence of values themselves."[7]

There is considerable pertinence in this estimate of Marquand's problem as an artist. The local traditions associated with New England village life, like that of the town of Clyde which represents one pole in so many of his novels, have been gradually disappearing under the pressures of technological change. The conclusion is documented by Marquand himself in his final book, a historical study of the changing conditions of life in his own village of Newburyport—the Clyde of the novels. *Timothy Dexter, Revisited* (1960) is a complete rewriting of an earlier study, undertaken in the 1920's, of a locally famed eccentric of the late eighteenth century named Timothy Dexter. No doubt the reason for "revisiting" Timothy Dexter, thirty-five years after his first study, was Marquand's need to understand what had happened to all the promise inherent in that golden past—to find, if possible, some explanation for the eclipse of a sturdy individualism —even an eccentric individualism like that of Timothy Dexter— by a split-level conformity. The reader of Marquand would probably find the character of Dexter less interesting than the detailed, nostalgic re-creation of a vanished past and the rather obvious lament for a more orderly and stable tradition, despite the urbane tone of Marquand's prose and his own disclaimer of such an intention.

The rags-to-riches career of Marquand's "Lord" Timothy Dexter, as he eventually called himself—who began as an indigent tanner and ended as the proud possesser of a wildly extravagant mansion in the center of the town, who even boasted his own poet laureate—stands in striking contrast to the unimaginative, colorless social pattern of contemporary Newburyport—or of contemporary America. In the end George Apley had asked himself, "I wonder will I walk up any road alone?" Marquand apparently saw Timothy Dexter as one who lived in an era when it was still possible to maintain his own splendid, inviolate individualism while—despite, or perhaps because of, his eccentricities—remaining a part of his community. But the Marquand of 1960, of *Women and Thomas Harrow* and *Timothy Dexter, Revisited*, was not an Apley struggling, however futilely, to break free from the ties of convention. On the contrary, as Kazin points out, he was fighting "*for* conventions—standards of belief and behavior—that will allow him to function as a human being again in a world where beliefs are shared."[8]

"Where beliefs are shared!" We are more than ever struck today by the prescience of a writer like D. H. Lawrence who intuitively perceived the American writer's need to reconcile his freedom as an individual with his requirement of a "living, organic, *believing* community, active in fulfilling some unfulfilled, perhaps unrealized purpose."[9] Despite the satirical emphasis of most of his novels, Marquand recognized from the beginning that it was necessary for one to move easily and with assurance in an acceptable and recognizable cultural milieu. If the image of the individual protagonist was to be projected with conviction, that image had to be seen as a part of an established social pattern which reflected the individual's relationship as well as his resistance to the society. "Men are free when they are in a living homeland, not when they are straying and breaking away," Lawrence asserted. "Men are free when they are obeying some deep, inward voice of religious belief."[10] Men are *not* free, he declared, when they are always escaping to some western wilderness where community is nothing and lawless individualism is all. We are reminded of Thoreau's contention that the California gold fields with their scrabbling seekers for uncreative wealth are—from his vantage point of Concord, Massachusetts, or Walden Pond—three thousand miles closer to hell.

Marquand himself expressed in a 1957 essay a view similar to Lawrence's: ". . . no one can write well and deeply of scenes and people that one has observed as an outsider. It is necessary, in order to write well of them, to have participated in some measure in a region's life, thought and emotion."[11] It is necessary, as Lawrence contended, to be a member of a "living, organic . . . community. . . ."

What happens, however, when the familiar landmarks of community have disappeared? When one discovers he no longer shares significantly in a region's life, thought, and emotion? When the region has become so radically changed by forces, social and technological, that the conventions and traditions of the once familiar community are like ghostly spectres in a buried past? Perhaps, for a social novelist like Marquand, who has always rejected the tradition represented by the Ishmaels of American literature, the thing which happens is an admission of despair and defeat in the creation of a Thomas Harrow, a modern Ishmael in a Brooks Brothers suit.

II *Women and Thomas Harrow*

In his last novel Marquand's Thomas Harrow replies to the state trooper who has stopped at the scene of a barely averted motor accident in which the desperately despairing Harrow has for the moment assented to his own self-destruction: " 'Why, thanks,' Tom said. 'I can drive back alone all right.' In the end, no matter how many were in the car, you always drove alone." But in Thomas Harrow's world if one drove alone it was with the knowledge that one was quite alone indeed; the atomization of society had left no beliefs to be shared.

A number of years ago in an interview with Robert Van Gelder, Marquand revealed that he had been in love with and wanted to live in the past. He wanted to forget the present and its realities. The result was his series of romantic historical novels and a cloak-and-dagger drama titled *The Unspeakable Gentleman*. He was, he said, "in love with candle light and old ships." Then disillusion set in, for reasons which he never really made clear—at least, in Van Gelder's interview—about the year 1936 at the time he was writing *The Late George Apley*. Perhaps the tone of Apley reflects in some degree the disillusionment; Marquand declared, ". . . I've changed. Now, by God, I gag at the past. I've got so I can't stand antiques. . . . It is a revolution, a personal revolution."[12]

But Marquand did not, perhaps could not, tell the whole story. Whatever the personal reasons may have been for his "personal revolution," it is certain that the past never failed to stimulate his imagination and to shape the patterns of his fiction. His *Timothy Dexter, Revisited* is clearly the work of one much more interested in antiquarianism than in history. And his Thomas Harrow is a man given to collecting "fragments to shore against our ruins": George the Second candlesticks, Chippendale tables, Paul Revere pewter, three-pronged forks, pistol-handled knives. He has deserted the city and returned to the town of his youth— Clyde once more—where he has purchased the beautiful old house with its "prayer closet" which he declines to sacrifice for an additional bathroom. This house represents for him a form of cultural piety, a link with an ordered past in which sound architectural and moral values prevailed. Almost a kind of talisman, the house is essential to Tom Harrow in the preservation of any measured and orderly life of his own; it is a hedge against hysteria and the ultimate despair. For his life came increasingly to seem nothing more than a "shoddy road, decorated meretriciously . . . with plastic refreshment booths and overnight motels . . . places of temporary respite for temporary indulgence, but no more."

It is a Federalist house which Thomas Harrow has acquired back in Clyde; something more than a status symbol, it represents almost the only tie with traditions of the past available to him in the mid-twentieth century. For not even the church in which Tom Harrow had first been married can now represent any link with the past, so thoroughly has it taken on the values of Madison Avenue commercialism. As the young pastor declares to Harrow, "Seriously, we're both in show business, Mr. Harrow." It's necessary for the minister to face the fact of competition like everybody else, he recognizes. The parables of the New Testament are, after all, pretty entertaining, Mr. Godfrey, the young pastor, asserts—and one has to be entertaining to catch the public's attention. Tom Harrow agrees that he may be right, but to the best of his recollection they had never before been presented to him in just that light. " 'I know what you mean,' Mr. Godfrey said. 'Black leather on the Bible and all that sort of thing. You've got to sell religion, don't you agree, Mr. Harrow?' " Tom Harrow, listening to the eager young man, was more than ever aware of the theatre sign across the street, the two-tone cars passing, the adjoining liquor store, and a night club, "The Chez Nanette," a new addition to the roster of Clyde enterprises.

It is interesting to observe that Marquand's protagonists grow older from book to book, along with their author. Thomas Harrow in this last novel is an American playwright of the generation immediately preceding the Arthur Millers and the Tennessee Williamses. He, like Marquand himself, achieved financial success and a considerable measure of critical acclaim with his first effort. At fifty-four, married to his third wife and not entirely happy in the relationship, he has reached the critical period of self-doubt which must surely come to every creative individual when he questions his ability to build upon his past success and to achieve a crowning work of unquestioned merit.

Perhaps his return home to the New England town where he grew up, his acquisition of the costly old Federalist mansion, and his unexpressed desire to win the local recognition that the implied social inferiority of his youth had denied him were all part of the uncertainty, were reflections of the troubled self-examination which followed the middle-aged questioning of the values by which he had lived and achieved his success. That success had come too easily to him. His first play, written and produced in the early 1920's, was titled *Hero's Return*. It had been witty, urbane, unusually polished for such a young playwright, and its sardonic tone caught the temper of the time. No one tells a success story better than Marquand, and the reader follows the spiralling success of young Tom Harrow with something of the fascination the giddy progress of a Fitzgerald hero elicits. Harrow's success permits him to marry Rhoda, the daughter of an unsuccessful automobile dealer and of his ambitious wife who has never ceased to feel superior to her well-meaning, lower middle-class husband.

Rhoda is one of Marquand's more unforgettable creations. The memory of her remains as real to the reader as it does to Tom Harrow. The first successful play is followed by others, and Tom and Rhoda are sought out and cultivated by the best representatives of the highest society. This success was for Tom Harrow, as for Rhoda, like a fairy tale for one who, like his creator, could not escape the conviction that environment was everything. But perhaps because it did all seem such a fabulous unreality to him, he sought always to maintain his ironic reservations about this easy success. He spent lavishly, even recklessly, and sought to obtain for Rhoda the extravagant status symbols of success.

It was not enough. Rhoda had never forgotten the pinch of poverty which she had known in youth. Neither had she forgotten the ambitious drive for security, for status and prestige, which she inherited from her mother. Harrow in Europe, enjoying the war and trying to believe that some features of man's estate are real and earnest, received word that Rhoda had left him for real security and patrician money—not that derived from a series of giddy successes on Broadway.

On the rebound and perhaps as a chivalric gesture immediately after the receipt of Rhoda's "Dear Tom" letter, Tom married the successful actress with whom he'd had an affair. A mistake from the beginning, the marriage lasted only briefly; however, the chivalrous Tom Harrow gave his second wife as generous a settlement as he had given Rhoda, though neither needed his generosity. His third wife, an actress on the verge of failure in the theatre, had little in common with Tom Harrow, the successful but improvident playwright. She found it difficult to follow the disturbing moods of her husband and regretted that he apparently found greater satisfaction in the hours spent in the company of his faithfully efficient secretary than those he had of necessity to spend with her.

In an effort to improve his fortune, Tom Harrow had invested in a musical comedy with a historical setting, a cloak-and-dagger affair. When the production proved an abysmal failure, Tom Harrow found himself on the verge of bankruptcy; his holdings in the market had been sold to meet his obligations. Such is his situation as the novel opens; the events which led to his present crisis provide, in the Jamesian sense, the subject of the tale. His third wife, fearing she will be left alone and without security, turns bitterly against him. His first wife, Rhoda, learning of his plight, has decided that perhaps she has not really been happy with a dull husband after all, despite her security; and she invites Tom Harrow to meet her at the rural resort hotel where they had spent their honeymoon so many years before. Perhaps, she suggests, if he wishes it, she might return to him, along with the whole generous settlement he had bestowed upon her. But Tom Harrow knows that it is quite as impossible to recapture that period of the past as it is to restore the Newburyport of the Federalist period. The conclusions to be drawn from *Thomas Harrow* and Marquand's nonfiction study of an older New England in *Timothy Dexter, Revisited* are the same. As he writes in the latter book, ". . . no past can ever return. There is no use weeping over things that are gone. They can never be retrieved in their ancient combinations." It was a greater Newburyport then, he feels confident, a greater town than it is now a city, with a more thoroughly cultivated citizenry —at least in the upper levels of that society—and "its inhabitants were more skilled in more crafts and more diligent in their work and worship."

Whatever, then, may have been the causes which turned Marquand against the past at the time he was writing *The Late George Apley*, those causes clearly did not persist in the shaping of the books to follow, for the tone of nostalgia for an unreclaimable past grows more pervasive from one book to another as the satirical sharpness declines. We are quite aware of the elegiac note in Marquand's final book; he leaves us in no doubt in *Timothy Dexter* concerning the choice he makes in his evaluation of past and present: ". . . the Newburyport of Dexter's day had as much or more than any other American community could then offer. The same cannot be said of it at present, nor of any of its prototypes along the New England seaboard."

We recognize, of course, that in all of the novels—at least, from *Pulham* to the last—the satire is less incisive than some readers might wish and that Marquand is obviously a man of divided mind; he admires the gentlemanly qualities and the traditional values manifested by a Pulham but questions their relevance in the modern world. Probably Marquand himself was never quite sure what he thought of Pulham as a character, and this tentativeness of judgment clearly mars the work as a satirical portrait. On the other hand, however, this very ambiguity of purpose may be responsible for giving us a work which is thoroughly representative of the mid-century with its troubled relativity of judgment. It is difficult to see how the times could have produced the incisive work of satire demanded by many critics, in view of the absence of a traditional pattern of values as a basis for comparison—the presence of a kind of knowledge of which even an Apley of an earlier generation had been half-aware.

Marquand, writing in the *Atlantic* in 1957, comments upon the treachery of Bill King and Kay Pulham as a factor which contributes substantially to the tragic implication of the book. And yet at the same time, perhaps without quite realizing the implication of his statement, he suggests that he may not have quite resolved the essential quality of Pulham's character even for himself. "In this regard," he writes, "there is one point of which I was not sure when I was writing the book and on which today I can still render no definite decision. Harry Pulham, in spite of an obviousness and a perennial desire for conformity, which must have been exasperating to his wife, was also endowed with considerable perceptive sentiment. Did he suspect this liaison, and did he stifle his suspicions out of loyalty or out of a wise reluctance to face the repercussions which might ensue? I am not sure, but I rather hope it was the latter."[13] Granted that Marquand no doubt wrote retrospectively with tongue in cheek, the statement nonetheless reveals more than was perhaps intended of the divided mind of John P. Marquand, torn between his own nostalgic longing for a better ordered past and his realistic recognition of a need for present compromise.

Alfred Kazin declares it must be apparent of Marquand's experience that he "has gone through the same helplessness before the defeat of the past, before the gradual extinction of our old American world, which he once satirized in the helplessness of Apley. And the more he has been forced to write from a point of view too reminiscent of naked experience, the more Marquand has softened and saddened, to the point where all satiric edge eventually disappears from *Women and Thomas Harrow*."[14] It is a conclusion with which we find it quite impossible to disagree. The nostalgia has got out of hand in this novel: and with so little satiric edge to create a balance of tone and to save the book from a kind of self-indulgent excess of feeling, we are aware of a quality of softness and a mounting sense of almost hysterical despair.

Yet the book does not fail to make its sharp and pointed indictments of contemporary America. But its protagonist is a man who came to maturity in the 1920's and whose values belong to an even earlier period. Marquand, certainly one of the successors of Howells as a novelist of "middle-browism" in America, is as a social observer quite as acute a critic in this novel as he had been earlier. But this Tom Harrow is, as a character, a reflection of all the doubts which afflict the modern man of good will resulting from the recognition of the past's inaccessibility and the present's vulgarity.

Richard Chase pointed out in his thoughtful study of *The American Novel and its Tradition* that ". . . many of the best American novels achieve their very being, their energy and their form, from the perception and acceptance not of unities but of radical disunities."[15] Precisely so. But as the disunities of our own time have become more apparent, the role of the social novelist has become increasingly untenable. It may have been possible, indeed, it may be possible now, for the American novelist to resolve the contradictions of our culture, as Mr. Chase contends, "in melodramatic actions or in pastoral idyls"; but such a solution was quite unthinkable for a novelist like Marquand who, perhaps more closely related to the English tradition in the novel than to the American, sought the middle way and the moral centrality of a viable tradition. If Marquand tended to reject the characters of Steinbeck, Faulkner, and

Hemingway because "they were never like anyone I knew," it is the result of his preference for the middle way, the English tradition, the "middle-browism" of the great English novelists from whom he descends—from Jane Austen and Thackeray and Trollope. The "radical disunities" of American life must finally fail to provide a theme for the social novelists, who must order the present by finding in the past a meaningful order and significance, a standard of values which can be drawn upon as a measure and balance for the highly relativistic and shifting standards of present-day American life. Perhaps for this reason Marquand was almost compulsively forced back, in the final work of his lifetime, to "revisit" the Federalist world of "Lord" Timothy Dexter. For had he not despairingly confessed in his examination of the fictional life of Thomas Harrow that for him time had ceased to convey a usable measure of the present? His narrator remarks: "The late Dr. Albert Einstein, or others vaguely in the Einstein category, had advanced the theory that time, being immaterial, was indestructible—and perhaps it was. . . . Yet, granted that the past was indestructible, exactly where was it now? Was it in good order, in keeping with the theories of relativity? He did not believe it was. The past in his experience was in a tangled mess like ticker tape."

Perhaps it might be said that Marquand is only one of the most recent American novelists in a continuing tradition to have arrived at similar conclusions. We suggest that Mr. Kazin may be begging the question when he speaks of "the intellectual poverty" of such a statement regarding past and present time and asserts that, after all, there is only one place where "the past ever makes sense—inside the creative human mind." We may assent to the last observation while questioning the validity of, or a possible alternative to, the statement that "To yield this [the creative human mind] to the American complaint that society has changed too much is to show up cruelly our lack of connection with ourselves."[16]

Certainly, such a lack of connection, whether cruelly revealed or not, is no new thing. Even Herman Melville (whom Marquand refers to in his final novel as "the great god of literature in America") demonstrates a not dissimilar concern with deliverance from time with his proposition, stated first in *Pierre*, that heavenly and earthly times are irreconcilable, that man is the great "chronometer" whereas God is a "horologue." And surely his creative life ended with the painful revelation of "our lack of connection with ourselves." His faith in the American tradition evinced in his works of the 1840's seems to have been pretty thoroughly eclipsed by the time he had completed his long philosophical poem *Clarel*. And to Melville's Bartleby the scriviner, the past might well have seemed like a "tangled mess of ticker tape," or, perhaps more appropriately, a "tangled mess of business ledgers and account books."

Perhaps the social novel in America, as it has been understood in the English tradition, was never really possible from the beginning. It is questionable, for example, that class and status have ever been firmly enough established and widely enough recognized in American society to provide the novelist of social relationships the kind of vantage point necessary for depicting people divided by class, or rising above class while being, at the same time, not "unconvincingly free of class." Without the sense of social propriety associated with a measure of stability assured by class, it may be quite impossible for the American novelist to avoid the description of a purely personal crisis. In any case, there is some basis for these doubts in the work of American writers (to name but two) like Henry James and Henry Adams. It might almost appear that the state of affairs for which Mr. Kazin has expressed regret in his *Atlantic* review-article of 1958 is, indeed, the inevitable fate of the serious writer in America.

One must believe in the imagination, Mr. Kazin asserts, since the imagination alone provides the means for our deliverance from time; and Tom Harrow, who was a thoroughly decent fellow, thoroughly aware of mortality in his fifty-fourth year, doesn't believe in the imagination any more "because his very facility as a writer has made him suspect the imagination." There is foundation for the assumption; Tom Harrow *does* suspect the facility which he has gained over the years, and he *does* conclude that it is not enough. He *does* share the self-doubts about the imagination with his fictional predecessors in Marquand's gallery: Jim Calder of *Wickford Point*, Jeffrey Wilson of *So Little Time*. As the latter character, while thinking of what was permanent, came to realize nothing really remained, "except perhaps personal relationships, but even these kept changing. You clung to beliefs and people and yourself, but even these kept changing." Now, fifteen years later, Tom Harrow becomes the Marquand character who expresses with a flat finality the inadequacy of the imagination as a solution to the purely personal existential problem.

He had been dealing all his life with the delicate fabrics of make-believe. His mind could touch them as the fingers of a connoisseur could touch the glazes of Chinese porcelain and judge their weights and values, but he was weary of exaggeration. For years there was always someone to laugh dutifully when he exercised his wit, but in the end, unless you were a moron, you had to know yourself.

In the end, of course, it was probably quite impossible to escape that "purely personal crisis." And we feel that finally, in the 1950's, it was Marquand's crisis as well. If the satirical edges of *Women and Thomas Harrow* are sometimes blurred, there is always a bitter bite in his observations of a contemporary world which, he almost seems to say, has value only for the "moron" who needs not know himself. Typically, he writes:

Everybody except dentists explaining toothbrushes smiled at everything. They smiled when they applied paste to their teeth; they smiled when they finally realized that various nationally advertised ingredients could rid them of excess perspiration and body odor. They smiled when they were suffering from mal-de-mer on the rear decks of cruise ships. One had to smile, even though the Caribbean, the Mediterranean and the Aegean, where burning Sappho loved and sang, were usually as turbulent as the British Channel. You had to smile because everything, including electric toasters and diaper services, was so enlightened in America.

The smiling problem was difficult for a woman, who now had to smile in a prefabricated way, with an elaborate dental finish, and when she smiled, her freshly polished teeth had to be in a conventional dental juxtaposition; and her lips, freshly kiss-proofed with a lipstick that would not come off no matter how hard she tried, had to be entirely symmetrical. Also, any good American woman, housewife or mother, when she smiled, had to have exquisitely but informally plucked eyebrows, and at the same time she had to roll her eyes sideways in a roguish but not immodest manner. She had to be a Pollyanna, the Glad Girl, even when she was in her girdle, or when the electrician came to fix the stove. It was immoral to admire a cross girl and most cross girls knew it.

The grotesqueries of the present serve always to remind Marquand of the inaccessibility of past time, or, more accurately, its absolute unrelatedness. When Harrow and his first wife Rhoda had visited Palm Beach with their new friends in the flush of their earliest Broadway success, the people had not been dull as they proved to be on his later visit. Then, in the years of youth, Lake Worth had not yet become a septic tank; the odor of American French fries and popcorn and frying fish did not permeate the atmosphere. "And what of the Ocean Boulevard," he wondered when he finally returned. "The Joe Davieses might still be there, and maybe the Kennedys," perhaps playing touch football on the expanse of lawn, but why, he asked himself, "did all the houses look like frosted cakes, and the palm trees and the pigeon plums and the Spanish bayonets and the hibiscus bushes appear grotesque?"

Nor, certainly, had New York escaped the vulgarization of the modern world. It was not now the genial and gracious city that he had first known. "Its taste for spaciousness and food and comfortable living had been dissipated. It had digested too many disparate and desperate people. It had contorted itself too often while struggling with its perpetual growing pains. Its manners, never good, had steadily deteriorated, along with its traffic and rapid transit." The new civic monuments, the Rockefeller centers, had more brashness than beauty. The few remaining brownstones were "mere faint memories of yesterday."

The conclusion which Tom Harrow arrived at—and it is essential Marquand, which might have application to all the other novels and to each of his principal characters in some degree—was that "there was no safety in living, and in the end, about all you got out of life was learning how to face truth without sidestepping to avoid it." Tom Harrow faced an increasing number of these truths as he approached the end of his career, not the least of which was the recognition that imagination and facility with words were not enough. He believed that he knew something of the principles underlying writing, knew them better than "the average professor of literature or drama," which was natural enough, since the professor preparing his lectures and writing his doctoral thesis spoke eloquently of literature and life without appreciating how far "life itself diverged from the printed page or the spoken line of the theatre. Writing was a heady brew, but it was never life itself. . . .There were a great many clever people who did not know what life was about, but the audience had to know the meaning when you wrote the show."

Women were a problem to Tom Harrow. It seemed to him that the world was less troubled when women thought less about their "manifest destiny" than they did at present—when they thought less about the necessity of integrating husband and children into the "togetherness" of the home, aided by ceaseless streams of marriage manuals and the counsels of sexologists of the press. "It now seemed to Tom that all through his life women—that is, good women—took themselves more seriously each year. . . ." He had grown increasingly to distrust the bedside books in "plain paper wrappers" by authorities in the medical and university world who could tell one exactly what to do in and out of bed, how to be patient, how to overcome frigidity, how to combat impotence, and, in fact, how to understand that sex could be fun as well as beautiful. "After his first encounter with this five-foot between-the-sheets library, he had not enjoyed it. . . ."

He reflected that, in the world he was sharing with a later generation, in his fifty-fourth year both he and the late D. H. Lawrence, whose *Lady Chatterley's Lover* had appeared, "would have blushed at the antics of characters subsequently dreamed up by the young hopes of American literature." Joyce's *Ulysses* (note particularly the subconscious reveries of Molly Bloom between waking and sleeping!) would seem pallid enough stuff now that sexual aberrations were old hat! And what had become of Trollope and William Makepeace Thackeray, figures now to be "passed off with a nervous shrug in a small Ivy League lecture room"? Tom Harrow could not forget the pertinence of *Vanity Fair,* with its description of Napoleon's advancing armies, "a quiet, old-fashioned and stilted passage" which still remained sound on the occasion when, in another drawing room amidst the "lilt of voices, and in the banality of the champagne humor," Tom Harrow, and America, prepared to go to war.

The examples provided are perhaps sufficient in number to show the dissatisfaction which Marquand's character felt with the cultural patterns of modern America. Tom Harrow, like Marquand himself, had been written about by a "bright young man" from the *New Yorker* in one of the magazine's "Profiles." In the article he had been called "the affable Mr. Harrow," and he wondered what it meant: did it refer to one with a "placating manner," or a "Dale-Carnegie-calculated drive to make friends and influence people, or merely proper manners? You never could tell how contemporary taste might succeed in warping the meaning of a word."

Life for Tom Harrow had become a "long day's journey into

night," and while it was desirable, certainly, to know oneself, it often seemed to him that "possibly all that anyone could do, in spite of the help of religion and of healers of the mind, was to have a polite, respectful bowing acquaintance with the ego, a sort of relationship that did not permit heart-to-heart discussions or true confessions." Perhaps, in short, the stoic way was best after all.

There is a great, and perhaps almost an inevitable temptation, to read *Women and Thomas Harrow* as an autobiographical confession—dangerous as such a reading might be to critical objectivity. For there is little doubt that the creative if not the emotional problems of the novel must have been John Phillips Marquand's quite as much as Thomas Harrow's. Tom hears his third wife bitterly charge that he has repeated himself in his work for the past five years; he concludes that the older one gets, the more desirous one is "to escape from truth and revelation because one learned that they were increasingly incontrovertible." And we are sure that both character and author might have been "careless with human relationships and with money, but never about his work, at least when he was working, and they could put it on his tombstone if they wanted."

Women and Thomas Harrow is a remarkable novel, particularly if read as the literary last will and testament of John P. Marquand. It reads almost as though he were aware (so dominant is the note of mortality in the novel) that he was, as Tom says, "on his way toward that bourne they wrote about and that one fact, after birth, that was completely unescapable. These were obvious facts, but now there was an urgent reminder that . . . he, too, was a part of the big parade. The younger generation, the younger writers, were waiting for him to pass the stand in review. Time was gently nudging so that he would make room for someone else. The show was never over, but pregnancy was continuing, drums were beating, and you had to march along."

It is not a bad note to end on; and if the past could never be recaptured, if the rupture between past and present had become so extreme that it could never be healed, then there was still the quiet conviction expressed by Tom Harrow, and perhaps by John Marquand as well, when he stood in the chapel of the First Congregational Church of Clyde that "he felt closer to truth there than he ever had at Notre Dame or Chartres. The thing that was called the New England conscience was in the cool silence, not reproof, but conscience."

That "conscience," a kind of ingrained personal integrity, came close to being very nearly the only thing Harrow had left. He recognized the universal appeal in the desire to return to old scenes. And very near the end of his personal drama, realizing that he has no resolution for his third act, he almost drives his chrome-plated, "nearly self-thinking automobile" through the guardrail into eternity. But he is too good a playwright, finally, to settle for an easy melodramatic ending, for a *deus ex machina.* He was returning from the fateful meeting with his first wife Rhoda at the rural hotel where they had spent their honeymoon so many years before. His own particular homecoming, his return to the past, had proved inevitably a failure. And he felt of himself that he was Ulysses driving up the road "through an Ithaca of his own contriving." Though the landmarks were vaguely familiar, ". . . the present was part of another day which gave the past impossibility, and this sense of unfamiliarity was most unpleasant because it made him feel that he was not identifiable with the new age." It was never a good idea to attempt a return, Harrow concludes. It was better to live with the memory. For finally one had to recognize that life was a game "in which you threw the dice just once."

In concluding, we must return once more, briefly, to the charge made by Alfred Kazin which has been considered in the opening pages of the present chapter. *Women and Thomas Harrow* certainly provides documentation enough of the "purely personal crisis" through which Harrow, as spokesman for Marquand, passes. But once assent is given to the proposition that the social novelist now "finds himself crying out against the absence of values themselves," as Mr. Kazin has asserted, it may be pointed out that we could hardly expect a social novelist, sensitive to the cultural patterns of the milieu of which he is a part, to escape that personal involvement which Mr. Kazin reprehends.

Perhaps what is required of the critic is a willingness to recognize that one must not define literary terms and genres too narrowly. If Jane Austen's relatively stable society appears to have little in common with Marquand's fluid and ceaselessly changing culture, the fact is perhaps not so important as that the social novelist in both periods shares the conviction that manners of an age must be evaluated—and perhaps corrected— in terms of some fixed and absolute standard of value, order, and traditional pattern. It must be said for Marquand that, even though he may cry out against the absence of values everywhere, those values are nonetheless real to him; and they continue to remain, in the midst of contemporary indifference, valid standards of measurement and of moral judgment.

The essential point is probably that, in the adaptation of the social novel or novel of manners to American conditions, we must find one pole of a bipolarity in the principles associated with what others have termed the American Faith: the pursuit of life, liberty, and happiness, the "rule of law." It is a faith which is personalist, a nonegoistic individualism, which seeks a balance between the individual and the community of which he is a part. The other pole is that representing an uncurbed, indifferent, highly relativistic individualism, which sacrifices every spiritual democratic value to an utterly rapacious and blind materialism. Understood in this sense, the basic conflict within American society is clearly enough seen, and Henry David Thoreau provided the ideological foundation upon which our latter-day social novelists were to build their interpretations of our society. Certainly, both John Phillips Marquand and James Gould Cozzens demonstrate again and again that most men lead lives of quiet desperation and that the "cost of a thing is the amount of what I call life which is required to be exchanged for it, immediately or in the long run." That was Thoreau's standard of value; it is, as well, the truth which Marquand's heroes and heroines are constantly discovering. And it is unlikely that a better summation of the meaning implicit in *Sincerely, Willis Wayde* could be found than that expressed by Thoreau when he wrote that ". . . trade curses everything it handles; and though you trade in messages from heaven, the whole curse of trade attaches to the business."

In Marquand's America the symbols of the old order, the old tradition, and the old stability were still there; but dominating and even overwhelming them were the constantly shifting and unstable signs of the new. If we see Marquand in terms of the polarities which represent his pattern, he is certainly a social novelist of distinction in the American tradition. In the following passage from *Women and Thomas Harrow*, detailing a series of significant contrasts, we may see illustrated the polarities I have set forth above:

> The small towns were still there, with their churches, and their houses grouped to express an older tradition. But the motor road was broader, and the main streets of the towns were cluttered with a conglomeration of parked cars with which he had no

sympathy. The elm trees which lined the streets were dying from a disease, and their dead limbs were like the bones of the past. Yet there was a note of hope. There was always a note of hope. The brave days of an age to come already formed a variegated carpet along the highway. Personally, he could call this carpet mediocrity, but doubtless he was wrong. Some people must have liked the hideous braided rugs dangling from lines to attract the motorist. Some people must have felt at home in the tangle of traffic, and in the cars, as sportive to his eyes as the ending of a new geological species. Some people must have liked the clusters of small new homes sown along the road like dragons' teeth. Some people must have liked them, since the inhabitants of these new homes, judging from the play yards and the juvenile wash upon the lines, had been indulging very freely in procreation. Then there were the new flat schools to house the product: and kennels selling pups—everybody in that brave new world must have been a dog lover; and driving ranges where one could hit golf balls; and motels that looked like Washington's Mount Vernon, or like a collection of Swiss chalets; and cocktail lounges, giant steaks and grand-slam cocktails. They expressed a part of a wish that was not always material, an aspiration that had always been a part of his country—Life, Liberty and the Pursuit of Happiness.

In the past, he had remembered, the region was one in which there was "sunlight and the scent of spruce and a feeling of country stretching on either side of them, in which anything might happen." If it was no longer true, there was still that "hope" —even though it was not one in which he, personally, could believe with much conviction. But always there was the need to hold on to the faith that perhaps this, poor as it seemed, was after all a recognizable pursuit of Life, Liberty and Happiness. Even at the end Harrow and Marquand were reluctant to deny the possibility that something might yet come from that "brave new world."

III *A Final Note*

In writing about Marquand today, we become aware that his work spanned a period and spoke for a generation that was perhaps the last to assert the validity of a set of values which were real even though they were most commonly conceived as remembrances of things past. The novel in the tradition of Conrad and James came to an end with the death or decline of writers like Marquand and his contemporaries. Marquand in particular, as a novelist of manners, is a transitional figure; and the younger writers who came after him at home and abroad have most often been spokesmen for what one critic has called "the new nihilism." We remember the oft-quoted words of Conrad's character, Stein in *Lord Jim*: "In the destructive element immerse." The way is to submit the self to the destructive element, "and with the exertions of your hands and feet in the water make the deep, deep sea keep you up. So if you ask me—how to be? . . . I will tell you! . . . In the destructive element immerse." Conrad, no less than James, saw the spectre of nothingness, the ghosts in the "Jolly Corner," but he persisted in his belief in "Fidelity," the foundation, according to Conrad, upon which the temporal world was based. And fidelity is the answer which the embattled individual spirit gives to the menacing spectre of nothingness, of corruption and evil.

Walter Allen asks, while writing of this problem as viewed by Conrad: "But what happens to a man when the barrier breaks down, when the evil without is acknowledged by the evil within, and fidelity is submerged?"[17] It all sounds very old-fashioned. Most of the younger novelists writing today could provide the answer: *There is no fidelity.* James's character in the remarkable late short story of "The Jolly Corner" discovers the tragic integration of the outer and the inner evil, but he is saved by the fidelity of the woman who has loved him through his years of nonrecognition (as other Jamesian characters—like the protagonist of "the Beast in the Jungle"—are not saved, and look upon nothingness when they reject this fidelity which might have saved them from their inescapable alienation). Of Lord Jim in the novel of that name, Marlowe, Conrad's narrator (and presumably Conrad himself), says that he was "one of us."

Such a recognition marks and distinguishes the novel which perhaps came to its final breath with writers of Marquand's generation. The novel of the first half of the twentieth century, particularly in England and America, might well be said to have restated again and again the Arnoldian thesis of "Dover Beach." With the decline of faith, the value became "let us be true to one another," since the world had "neither joy, nor love, nor light, nor certitude, nor peace, nor help for pain. . . ." Finally, the tradition raveled out, and the end of the tether was reached in Hemingway's Colonel Cantwell of *Across the River and Into the Trees;* an aging soldier and an extraordinarily pliant young countess fornicate in gondolas and look obliquely into the yawning mouth of nothingness. *Nada nada* has come at last—in the kingdom and the glory of *nada*.

In America, of course, as Norman Podhoretz pointed out some time back, concern regarding the loss of values has in recent years become "a received idea, a cliché, and the best anyone could do with it was to trot out mechanical symbolic allusions. . . ."[18] The rejection of ideologies, as Daniel Bell has so brilliantly set forth in his recent essay,[19] has been accompanied by the loss of passion. It is no new thing, either, for the prophet to point out that "Things fall apart; the centre cannot hold; Mere anarchy is loosed upon the world," or to tell us "poor wanderers between faith and doubt," as Conrad Aiken did years ago, that if we need a theme "then let that be our theme."

But if the modern novel's iteration of the theme of lost values hardly comes to us with the freshness of discovery, we cannot fail to note the funk, on the one hand, or the almost complete nihilistic rejection of the possibility of value, ethical and humanistic, on the other. As Podhoretz observed, "it was Camus who first spotted the significance of this new style of nihilism and identified it, in *The Stranger,* with the pathological apathy of the narrator Meursault—the French were far in advance of the Americans in seeing that the 'rebel' was giving way in our day to the 'stranger.' "[20] This development in the modern novel truly marks the line dividing the writers of an earlier generation from those who have followed the lead of Camus; they, looking at the world and into themselves, have discovered nothingness.

Conrad, no less than the younger writers of the present generation, rejected the conventional ideologies of church and state, and yet there was meaning for him in his continuing acceptance of the innate tragic nobility of man's lonely struggle. As Ernest A. Baker wrote, Conrad, while rejecting all the supernaturalistic creeds, found his religion in "his realization of man's uniqueness and loneliness in an indifferent and inscrutable universe, the acute sense of man's dignity and man's self-responsibilty, and a sense, equally acute, equally profound, not merely of abstract justice, but of the superlative value to man of courage, endurance, and loyalty to his fellowmen. . . ."[21] Conrad, and other major writers of his generation, continued to believe in the virtue and the possibility of rebellion; the rebel had not yet given away to the stranger. Creation, he asserted in *A Personal Record,* may never aim at ethical conclusions at all (indeed, any ethical view might well prove utterly false), but at pure spectacle, "a spectacle for awe, love, adoration, or hatred, if you like, but in this view—and in this view alone—never for despair. . . . The unwearied self-forgetful attention to every phase of the living universe may be our appointed task on this earth."[22]

And so fidelity, the virtues of courage, endurance, and loyalty, continued to serve as the armor in the struggle against the spectre of nothingness arising from the dark. Such concern for the virtues associated with the idea of such fidelity is present in the novels of Marquand, and it places him in the tradition of an earlier generation which finds it possible, even necessary, to resist any submission to the nothingness and the meaninglessness of existence.

To say as much, of course, is not to suggest that Marquand is at all the kind of novelist Conrad was. Marquand's world is quite a different one; the rebellions of his characters are quieter, less openly dramatic, though certainly no less poignant. It seems not unlikely that Marquand has won and retained a large following in the United States as a result of his rather stubborn insistence that some standards may be maintained in a world which appears willing to reject any such possibility. At a time when all conventions have been treated as anachronistic survivals which should long ago have lain down decently and given up the ghost, Marquand's readers are grateful for a voice which continued to insist, rather feebly at times, no doubt, that the Arnoldian doctrine is not yet moribund, that decency and loyalty and courage have a place in life, and that some standards are capable of informing the cultural patterns of our day. If, as has been asserted, it is in our day quite impossible to proclaim the absolute dedication to a moral code, Marquand provides the next best possibility—something, to be sure, less than a moral code with absolute finality; but in lieu of a code, we have at least a sense of fidelity to standards reaffirmed, even if often more honored in the breach than in the observance.

Notes and References

Chapter One

1. Irving Howe, "Mass Society and Post-Modern Fiction," *Partisan Review*, XXVI, No. 3 (Summer, 1959), 426.
2. *Ibid.*, p. 432.
3. Philip Hamburger, *John P. Marquand, Esquire* (1952), p. 7.
4. Cited by Charles A. Brady, "John Phillips Marquand: Martini-Age Victorian," *Fifty Years of the American Novel: A Christian Appraisal*, ed. Harold C. Gardiner, S. J. (1951), p. 107.
5. *Ibid.*, p. 109.
6. *Ibid.*, pp. 115-16.
7. Nathan Glick, "Marquand's Vanishing American Aristocracy: Good Manners and the Good Life." *Commentary*, IX (1950), 435.
8. W. J. Smith, "J. P. Marquand, Esq.," *Commonweal*, LXIX (Nov. 7, 1958), 150.
9. Glick, p. 440.
10. *Ibid.*, p. 441.
11. Leo Gurko, "The High Level Formula of J. P. Marquand," *American Scholar*, XXI, No. 4 (October, 1952), 443-44.
12. *Ibid.*, p. 448.
13. *Ibid.*, p. 451.
14. Randall Jarrell, "Very Graceful are the Uses of Culture," *Harper's Magazine*, CCIX (November, 1954), 94. Mr. Jarrell makes his comments in his review of Marquand's collection of short stories and articles, *Thirty Years*, and uses the opportunity to express some judgments about Marquand's work as a whole.
15. *Ibid.*, p. 96.
16. *Ibid.*
17. Alfred Kazin, "John P. Marquand and the American Failure," *Atlantic Monthly*, CCII, No. 5 (November, 1958), 153.
18. The lecture appears in his collected short pieces, *Thirty Years*. The lecture and article, dated 1949, is titled "A Discussion of the Novel."
19. Mr. Fadiman's comments appear in his introduction to Marquand's *Thirty Years*.

Chapter Two

1. Fadiman, Introduction to *Thirty Years*, p. 12.
2. The writer obviously intended to acknowledge by the use of his subtitle, "A Novel in the Form of a Memoir," the precedent

Notes and References

"A Memoir in the Form of a Novel," George Santayana's *The Last Puritan.*

3. Joseph Warren Beach, *American Fiction: 1920-1940* (1941), p. 254.

4. John P. Marquand, "Apley, Wickford Point, and Pulham," *Atlantic Monthly,* CXCVIII (September, 1956), 72. The same material also appeared as introductions to the New England novels in the omnibus *North of Grand Central* (1956), with an introductory essay by Kenneth Roberts.

5. *Ibid.*

6. Beach, pp. 265-66.

7. Marquand, p. 72.

8. "Notes and Comment," *New Yorker* (August 6, 1960), p. 19.

9. In an anonymous tribute to Marquand following his death, *Time* (July 25, 1960), p. 77.

Chapter Three

1. John P. Marquand, "Hearsay History of Curzon's Mill," *Atlantic Monthly,* CC (November, 1957), p. 84.

2. It has generally been assumed that the model for old John Brill, sage of Wickford Point, was Edward Everett Hale: "the tribal fetish Marquand exasperatedly repudiates but which he cannot escape," as Charles Brady puts it. However, according to Mr. Brady, Marquand asserted that if any actual person was intended in the portrait of old Brill it was probably John Greenleaf Whittier. Marquand, though, would almost certainly have had a higher regard for the memory of Whittier than the Brill portrait would indicate—not to mention Whittier's single state and his abjuration of tobacco in any form. Philip Hamburger states (p. 102) that Whittier sometimes rowed across the river from Amesbury to read from his works to Marquand's Aunt Mary, "on whom he had a crush."

3. Joseph Warren Beach, *American Fiction: 1920-1940* (1941), p. 257.

4. Percy H. Boynton, *America in Contemporary Fiction* (1940), p. 51.

5. See Philip Hamburger, *John P. Marquand, Esquire,* for a report on the legal quarrels with his cousins the Hales, pp. 103-5.

6. Boynton, p. 52.

7. Beach, p. 258.

8. Maxwell Geismar, "John P. Marquand, the Writer," *Saturday Review,* XLIII, No. 33 (August 13, 1960), 15.

9. Edward Weeks, "John P. Marquand," *Atlantic Monthly,* CCVI, No. 4 (October, 1960), 75.

Chapter Four

1. Brady, p. 122.
2. Hamburger, *J. P. Marquand, Esquire*, p. 85.
3. Brady, p. 111.
4. *Ibid.*, p. 130.
5. *Ibid.*
6. Sinclair Lewis, *Babbitt* (New York: 1922), p. 386.

Chapter Five

1. See Philip Hamburger for these biographical details, *J. P. Marquand, Esquire*, 40-41.
2. Brady, p. 128.
3. *Ibid.*, p. 121.
4. Kazin, "John P. Marquand and the American Failure," p. 153.
5. *Ibid.*
6. *Ibid.*, p. 154.
7. Brady, p. 117.
8. *Ibid.*, p. 130.
9. Granville Hicks, "Marquand of Newburyport," *Harper's Magazine*, CC (April, 1950), 106.
10. Jarrell, "Very Graceful are the Uses of Culture," 95-96.
11. *Ibid.*, p. 96.
12. Gurko, "The High Level Formula of John P. Marquand," p. 445.
13. Brady, p. 119.
14. Gurko, p. 451.
15. See Philip Hamburger, *J. P. Marquand, Esquire*, pp. 26-32. One of Marquand's closest friends was Harvard classmate, George W. Merck, president of the pharmaceutical firm, who often visited Marquand on his rented Treasure Island just off Nassau. Hamburger writes: "Few writers ever came to Treasure Island, and if many had come, their talk, he was certain, would have driven him mad—especially the incessant din they would have set up about James, Fitzgerald, and Joyce" (p. 31). Marquand never met Hemingway or Faulkner, though he "regretted never having talked with Sherwood Anderson" (p. 31). An additional incident related by Hamburger is worth retelling. "He suddenly thought back to that day in Taormina, in the twenties, when a friend introduced him, in the lobby of his hotel, to a strange creature in sandals, with red hair, and sockets for eyes, whose name he didn't catch. They chatted for a while about Sicily, and the man said that he was living somewhere in the hills. The next day, Marquand's friend asked him what he had thought of·the odd-looking chap, and Marquand said, 'He is quite off his trolley. Who is he?' 'That was D. H. Lawrence,' his friend said. His friend later asked Lawrence what *he* thought of Marquand, and Lawrence said, 'The fellow is quite mad.' " (p. 31).

Chapter Six

1. Brady, p. 132.
2. *Ibid.*
3. Henry Hewes, "Mr. Marquand Turns a Point," *Saturday Review*, XXV (January 26, 1952), 22.
4. Hicks, p. 106.
5. Maxwell Geismar, *American Moderns: From Rebellion to Conformity* (New York, 1958), p. 158.
6. Joseph A. Kahl, *The American Class Structure* (1958), p. 24.
7. Hicks, p. 102.
8. Simon and Schuster, New York, 1958, pp. 38-39.
9. *Ibid.*, p. 271.

Chapter Seven

1. Geismar, *American Moderns: From Rebellion to Conformity*, p. 161.
2. Nathan Cosman, "Speakable Gentleman," *Nation*, CLXXXV (August 3, 1957), 56.
3. Brady, pp. 114-15.
4. Geismar, p. 160.
5. *Ibid.*
6. Crane Brinton, *The Shaping of the Modern Mind* (New York, 1957), pp. 15-16.

Chapter Eight

1. Geismar, pp. 161-62.
2. Edward Weeks, "John P. Marquand," *Atlantic Monthly*, CCVI, No. 4 (October, 1960), 76.

Chapter Nine

1. Kazin, "John P. Marquand and the American Failure," p. 156.
2. *Ibid.*
3. John Gunther, "A Quarter Century: Where Has it Left Us?," *Look Magazine* (January 2, 1962), p. 73.
4. *Ibid.*
5. Alfred M. Landon, as recently quoted in the press.
6. Kazin, p. 154.
7. *Ibid.*, p. 156.
8. *Ibid.*
9. D. H. Lawrence, *Studies in Classic American Literature*, (Garden City, New York: Doubleday Anchor Books, 1953), p. 17.
10. *Ibid.*
11. John P. Marquand, "Hearsay History of Curzon's Mill," *Atlantic Monthly*, CC (November, 1957), 73.
12. Robert Van Gelder, "An Interview with a Best-Selling Author: John P. Marquand," *Cosmopolitan*, CXXII (March, 1947), 150.

13. Marquand, "Apley, Wickford Point, and Pulham," p. 74.

14. Kazin, p. 154.

15. Richard Chase, *The American Novel and its Tradition*, (Garden City, New York, 1957), p. 7.

16. Kazin, p. 156.

17. Walter Allen, *The English Novel: A Short Critical History* (New York, 1955), p. 363.

18. Norman Podhoretz, "The New Nihilism and the Novel," *Partisan Review*, XXV, No. 4 (Fall, 1958), 576.

19. *End of Ideology* (Glencoe, Ill., 1959).

20. Podhoretz, p. 584.

21. Ernest A. Baker, *The History of the English Novel*, X (New York, 1950), 43-44.

22. Quoted in Allen, p. 363.

Selected Bibliography

PRIMARY SOURCES

Books

The Unspeakable Gentleman. New York: Charles Scribner's Sons, 1922.

Four of a Kind. New York: Charles Scribner's Sons, 1923. (A collection of four long stories.)

Black Cargo. New York: Charles Scribner's Sons, 1925.

Lord Timothy Dexter of Newburyport, Massachusetts. New York: Minton, Balch & Co., 1925. (New popular edition, New York: G. P. Putnam's Sons, 1935.)

Warning Hill. Boston, Toronto: Little, Brown and Company, 1930.

Haven's End. Boston, Toronto: Little Brown and Company, 1933.

No Hero. Boston, Toronto: Little, Brown and Company, 1935.

Ming Yellow. Boston, Toronto: Little, Brown and Company, 1936.

The Late George Apley. Boston, Toronto: Little Brown and Company, 1937. (Play version 1944 with George F. Kauffman.)

Think Fast, Mr. Moto. Boston, Toronto: Little, Brown and Company, 1937.

Mr. Moto is So Sorry. Boston, Toronto: Little, Brown and Company, 1938.

Wickford Point. Boston, Toronto: Little, Brown and Company, 1939.

H. M. Pulham, Esquire. Boston, Toronto: Little, Brown and Company, 1941. (English title, *Don't Ask Questions.* London: Robert Hale Limited, 1942.)

Last Laugh, Mr. Moto. Boston, Toronto: Little, Brown and Company, 1942.

So Little Time. Boston, Toronto: Little, Brown and Comany, 1943.

Repent in Haste. Boston, Toronto: Little, Brown and Company, 1945.

B. F.'s Daughter. Boston, Toronto: Little, Brown and Company, 1946. (English title, *Polly Fulton.* London: Robert Hale Limited, 1947.)

Point of No Return. Boston, Toronto: Little, Brown and Company, 1949. (Also play with Paul Osborne, 1951.)

Melville Goodwin, U.S.A. Boston, Toronto: Little, Brown and Company, 1951.

Thirty Years. Boston, Toronto: Little, Brown and Company, 1954.

Sincerely, Willis Wayde. Boston, Toronto: Little, Brown and Company, 1955.

North of Grand Central. Boston, Toronto: Little, Brown and Company, 1956. (An omnibus edition of *Apley, Wickford Point,* and *H. M.*

Pulham, Esquire, with commentary by Marquand and an intro-
duction by Kenneth Roberts.)
Stopover: Tokyo. Boston, Toronto: Little, Brown and Company, 1957.
Life at Happy Knoll. Boston, Toronto: Little, Brown and Company,
1957.
Women and Thomas Harrow. Boston, Toronto: Little, Brown and
Company, 1958.
Timothy Dexter Revisited. Boston, Toronto: Little, Brown and Com-
pany, 1960.

Articles of Particular Interest

"Apley, Wickford Point, and Pulham," *Atlantic,* CXCVIII (September,
1956), 71-74. Marquand's own reflections upon his first three
New England novels which reveal, consciously and unconsciously,
much about the inception of the works.
"Fitzgerald: *This Side of Paradise,*" *Saturday Review of Literature*
(Twenty-fifth Anniversary Issue, "Looking Backwards"), XXXII
(August 6, 1949), 30-31. A gracious tribute to a writer whose
work he much admired.
"Hearsay History of Curzon's Mill," *Atlantic,* CC (November, 1957),
84-91. Valuable to the student of Marquand for his own recollec-
tions of the area in Massachusetts—the setting of his novel
Wickford Point—where he spent his early years.
"Return Trip to the Stone Age," *Atlantic,* CLXXXIII (April, 1949),
25-28. The short journalistic report of a trip by Marquand to
the island of Truk, significant for his treatment of past time
since it reveals the quality of his imagination.

SECONDARY SOURCES

AMORY, CLEVELAND. *The Proper Bostonians.* New York: E. P. Dutton
& Co., 1947. Essential background for a better understanding of
Apley and the New England novels.
AUCHINLOSS, LOUIS. "Marquand and O'Hara: The Novel of Manners,"
Nation, CLXCI (November 19, 1960), 383-84. The basis for
class divisions becomes increasingly uncertain in Marquand's
novels, and, consequently, his characters become more indefinite
in outline as the basis for the social novel in America disappears.
BENÉT, STEPHEN AND ROSEMARY. "J. P. Marquand, A Really Remark-
able Writer." *New York Herald-Tribune Books,* XVII (March
16, 1941), 5. Warm praise for the new Marquand in *Apley.*
BISBEE, THAYER DONOVAN. "J. P. Marquand's Tales of Two Cities,"
Saturday Review of Literature, XXIV (July 5, 1941), 11-14.
Consideration of Marquand's treatment of New York and Boston
in *Pulham.*

BOYNTON, PERCY HOLMES. *America in Contemporary Fiction.* Chicago: University of Chicago Press, 1940. The first volume to give serious consideration to *Apley* and *Wickford Point.*

————. "The Novel of Puritan Decay: From Mrs. Stowe to John Marquand," *New England Quarterly,* XIII (December, 1940), 626-37. A chapter, "Puritanism in New England," in the volume named above.

BRADY, CHARLES A. "John Phillips Marquand: Martini-Age Victorian," in *Fifty Years of the American Novel,* ed. Harold C. Gardiner, S. J. (New York and London: Charles Scribner's Sons, 1951), pp. 107-34. Probably the soundest evaluation of Marquand's significance as a novelist, even though written before the last novels had appeared.

BRICKELL, HERSCHEL. "Miss Glasgow and Mr. Marquand," *Virginia Quarterly Review,* XVII (Summer, 1941), 405-17. ". . . not only two of the most civilized of our novelists, but two of the best of this or any other time." Mr. Brickell declares that "the only triumph possible in life is refusal to accept defeat"—a meaning attributed to Ellen Glasgow but implied also as regarding the work of Marquand.

BROWN, JOHN MASON AND MAXWELL GEISMAR. "John P. Marquand: The Man and the Writer," *Saturday Review,* XLIII (August 13, 1960), 14-15. Brief posthumous appreciations of the man by Brown, and of the writer by Geismar.

BURGUM, EDWIN BERRY. "American Sociology in Transition," *Science and Society,* XXIII (Fall, 1959), 317-32. An analysis of sociological studies with a comparison of the social criticism of Marquand and Wilson.

BUTTERFIELD, ROGER. "John P. Marquand: America's Famous Novelist of Manners," *Life,* XVII (July 31, 1944), 64-73. A primary source of biographical information.

COSMAN, N. "Speakable Gentleman," *Nation,* CLXXXV (August 3, 1957), 56-57. A review of *Life at Happy Knoll* in which the author maintains that Marquand is not fierce enough for a satirist. "To scorn and to embrace a subject alternately is not a virtue but an indulgence. . . . He attacks but never to the limit."

GEISMAR, MAXWELL. *American Moderns: From Rebellion to Conformity.* New York: Hill and Wang, 1958. Geismar reflects upon the reasons for the decline of Marquand's talent in the later years of his career and reprints reviews of *Point of No Return* and *Melville Goodwin, U.S.A.* He concludes that "Mr. Marquand knows all the little answers. He avoids the larger questions."

GLICK, NATHAN. "Marquand's Vanishing American Aristocracy: Good Manners and the Good Life," *Commentary,* IX (1950), 435-41. An essentially unsympathetic appraisal of Marquand and his work. He writes that "John Phillips Marquand is, alas, our most accomplished novelist of manners," and he regrets that Marquand was not a Proust.

GOODWIN, GEORGE, JR. "The Last Hurrahs: George Apley and Frank Skeffington," *Massachusetts Review*, I, 461-71. Both in their turn represented the last hurrahs of their respective traditions which had come to an end.

GURKO, LEO. "The High Level Formula of J. P. Marquand," *American Scholar*, XXI, 4 (October, 1952), 443-53. Though the pragmatic case of Marquand's reflections on larger issues exercises a strong attraction upon his readers, he is really bound to a formula, "a high-level formula in every sense, but with the rigid limits the word implies."

HALSEY, VAN R. "Fiction and the Businessman," *American Quarterly*, XI (Fall, 1959), 391-402. The concern for the individual of many contemporary novelists, Marquand included, results in a distorted view of the businessman.

HAMBURGER, PHILIP. *J. P. Marquand, Esquire*. Boston: Houghton Mifflin Company, 1952. A series of "profiles" which first appeared in *The New Yorker*, they won at least the limited approval of Marquand himself. Hamburger, writing in imitation of the Marquand style, has provided the student of Marquand with the fullest biographical treatment of the novelist to date.

HATCHER, HARLAN. "John Phillips Marquand," *College English*, I (November, 1939), 107-18; *English Journal*, XXVIII (September, 1939), 507-18. An early and necessarily incomplete evaluation of Marquand as a major and significant contemporary novelist.

HELLMAN, GEOFFREY T. "How to Take the World in Your Stride (After Being Tipped Off by J. P. Marquand)," *The New Yorker*, XVIX (October 22, 1943), 20-21. A parody in Marquand's style of the urgency associated with the war in *So Little Time*.

HEWES, HENRY. "Mr. Marquand Turns a Point," *Saturday Review*, XXXV (January 26, 1952), 22. A brief interview with Marquand regarding the treatment of the situation in *Point of No Return* in the dramatic version.

HICKS, GRANVILLE. "Marquand of Newburyport," *Harper's Magazine*, CC (April, 1950), 105-8. Certainly one of the two or three best essays on Marquand, and the first to recognize the great significance of his Newburyport background.

HOUGHTON, FREDERICK AND RICHARD WHITMAN. "J. P. Marquand Speaking," *Cosmopolitan*, CXLVII (August, 1959), 46-50. An interview which contains valuable biographical background and significant Marquand opinions.

JARRELL, RANDALL. "Very Graceful are the Uses of Culture," *Harper's Magazine*, CCIX (November, 1954), 94-95. Very graceful are the judgments of Jarrell. Mr. Jarrell's review of Marquand's

Thirty Years has some pertinent observations on Marquand's themes and compulsions.

KAHL, JOSEPH A. *The American Class Structure*. New York: Rinehart and Company, 1960. Professor Kahl's sociology text develops the F. Lloyd Warner thesis relating to the class structure of American society. His observations are of value in appraising the contribution of Marquand to an understanding of the changing class relationship in mid-century America.

KAZIN, ALBERT. "John P. Marquand and the American Failure," *Atlantic*, CCII (November, 1958), 152-54. Though ostensibly a review of Marquand's last novel, *Women and Thomas Harrow*, Kazin has written one of the most perceptive evaluations of Marquand's career and of the role of the social novelist in America which has yet appeared.

"Notes and Comments," *The New Yorker*, XXXVI (August 6, 1960), 19. A warm and generous tribute to Marquand following his death.

ROBERTS, KENNETH. "Memories of John P. Marquand," *Saturday Review*, XXXIX (September 15, 1956), 14-15. An excerpt from the introduction to Marquand's omnibus *North of Grand Central*.

SMITH, HARRISON. "Marquand Self Appraised," *Saturday Review*, XXXVII (November 27, 1954), 13. A review of *Thirty Years*.

SMITH, W. J. "J. P. Marquand, Esq." *Commonweal*, LXIX (November 7, 1958), 148-50. A review of *Thomas Harrow*. "Mr. Marquand builds a house that may fall into disfavor, but it will stand sturdy."

VAN GELDER, ROBERT. "Marquand Unburdens Himself," *New York Times Book Review* (April 7, 1940), 20-21. An understanding review of *Wickford Point*.

————."An interview with a Best-Selling Author: John P. Marquand," *Cosmopolitan*, CXXII (March, 1947), 18, 150-52. One of the better and more revealing interviews with Marquand, a primary source for biographical information.

Weeks, Edward. "John P. Marquand," *Atlantic Monthly*, CCVI (October, 1960), 74-76. An affectionate tribute to Marquand by a long-time friend.

White, William. "Mr. Marquand's Mr. Moto," *American Speech*, XXIII (April, 1948), 157-58. The speech of Mr. Marquand's most famous character.

————. "John P. Marquand: A Preliminary Checklist," *Bulletin of Bibliography*, XVIX (Sept.-Dec., 1949), 268-71.

————. "Marquandiana," *Bulletin of Bibliography*, XX (January, April, 1950), 8-12.

Whyte, William A., Jr. *The Organization Man*. New York: Simon and Schuster, 1956. An essential background book for an understanding of Marquand's business novels.

Index

Index